THEQUESTIONS

CONTENTS

This edition published in 2018 by Cavendish Square Publishing, LLC
243 5th Avenue, Suite 136, New York, NY 10016

Copyright © 2018 by Worth Press Ltd.

Additional end matter copyright © 2018 by Cavendish Square Publishing, LLC

First Edition

Website: cavendishsq.com

This publication represents the opinions and views of the author based on his or her personal experience, knowledge, and research. The information in this book serves as a general guide only. The author and publisher have used their best efforts in preparing this book and disclaim liability rising directly or indirectly from the use and application of this book.

All websites were available and accurate when this book was sent to press.

Library of Congress Cataloging-in-Publication Data

Names: Jackson, Tom.
Title: Life and death : why we are here and where we go / Tom Jackson.
Description: New York : Cavendish Square, 2017. | Series: The big questions | Includes index.
Identifiers: ISBN 9781502628107 (library bound) | ISBN 9781502628114 (ebook)
Subjects: LCSH: Life--Origin--Juvenile literature. | Death--Juvenile literature.
Classification: LCC QH325.J32 2017 | DDC 576.8'3--dc23

Editorial Director: David McNamara
Editor: Caitlyn Miller
Associate Art Director: Amy Greenan
Production Coordinator: Karol Szymczuk

Printed in the United States of America

LIFE AND DEATH

WHY WE ARE HERE AND WHERE WE GO

TOM JACKSON

Cavendish
Square

ew Yc

LIFE&DEATH

WHY WE ARE HERE AND WHERE WE GO

INTRODUCTION

> "We wonder if beating death will ever be possible and if it were whether any of us would bother to do it. "

Questions do not come bigger than those concerning life and death. Where did we come from and where are we going? Those are the two basic questions that underlie all of scientific inquiry and also fill the days of philosophers past, present, and future. The questions get their meaning from the fact we are alive, and want to continue living, but know that our death will arrive one day.

This book approaches answers to these questions from several different directions. It sets out what science has revealed—and what is still puzzled over—about the way life works and how it might have started. We take a look at consciousness and its role in our experience of death. We wonder if beating death will ever be possible and if it were whether any of us would bother to do it. Is death even the end? I'm afraid we will all just have to wait and see about that. That is, if we are even alive in the first place—there are suggestions that we may not be quite as alive as we think!

Q1
WHAT IS
LIFE?

We might as well start with the biggest one of all. And it might be easier to understand life by thinking about death. We can safely say that this book, the one you are reading now, is dead. Mostly. It is possibly a little bit alive, with lice and mites in its bindings, feasting on the glue. However, that is not really the point we need to make. The paper pages are dead. To be dead, something has to have been alive at some point. The paper is made from wood, the lignified cells of a pine tree that was once living, but then was cut down and pulped. So the paper is dead. What about the ink? The black ink is made from ultrafine carbon particles. They are extracted from the processing of petroleum, which is the remains of long dead microorganisms. So is the ink dead as well? We'd probably agree that it was not, since a great deal of time has elapsed since it was alive, and many processes have altered it sufficiently to be nothing like its original living form. However, this semantic point is not the one we want to pursue. Rather we are homing in on an idea that the universe is divided into two kinds of materials: inanimate ones that are derived from nonliving processes, and animate ones that are created by life.

> To be dead, something has to have been alive at some point.

Which one is alive, and which one is dead?

It is safe to say that the former group far outweighs the latter one. So what is the difference? According to one viewpoint, a living thing has to be made of cells—at least one and perhaps trillions. But that is more of an observation about the shared characteristics of life on Earth than a universal requirement of life. Just because life does not exist on this planet without cells, who is to say that life cannot ever exist without a cell? Well, whoever does say it must have some deeper understanding of what life is.

Another way of describing life is that it is a self-sustaining process, but that too is incomplete. There are other self-sustaining, self-regulating processes that are not alive. Examples could be the weather or the engine of a car.

"The shortest way of summing up life is "**merring**."

So we are forced to become more specific. There is no simple, ear-catching description of life. Quite the opposite, in fact. The shortest way of summing up life is "**merring**." It's not a word but an acronym. There are others, but they all say the same kind of things:

Movement

Excretion

Respiration

Reproduction

Irritability

Nutrition

Growth

Life on the move

Many of those terms are perhaps obvious, but the need for a second vowel in the mnemonic has thrown up the term irritability—does that mean living things are all grumpy? Obviously not, but let's start from the beginning.

Movement is perhaps easy to understand. You are doing it now, perhaps imperceptibly, but the heart is pumping, chest rising and falling, eyes blinking, and at a whim you could move any part of your body. So does that mean you are alive? Well, it is the first criterion on the list. But remember a car can move as well. Is that alive, too?

And what of other forms of life—a mushroom or tree? Here the concept of movement becomes more subtle. Certainly these organisms are not capable of locomotion like you or the car, but they do exhibit control over their body's position, albeit in very limited and rather passive ways. A tree can orientate its leaves to face toward the sun. Every plant leaf has a system of pores, called stomata, that open and close during the right conditions. Moss even produces sperm that swims through water with a wiggle of a tail in that familiar way.

> " Every plant leaf has a system of pores, called stomata, that open and close during the right conditions. "

> 66 There are carnivorous fungi that set snares for worms in the soil. 99

A mushroom is the fruiting body of a fungus, and this one is harder to give a pass mark in the movement test. Some fruiting bodies, puffballs are a good example, have elaborate spore dispersal systems that trigger when the conditions are right. Also, there are carnivorous fungi that set snares for worms in the soil. When the worm wriggles through, the fungal loop tightens. Goodbye worm. However, this type of motion is a real exception. In the end, we have to accept that movement at the very least is the ability to transfer the body, or at least a tiny part of it to a new location. In that case, the spore dispersal of a fungus qualifies as movement just as much as

A 2D view shows the gut is an external body surface.

the sprint of a cheetah. The cheetah can outpace a car from a standing start over 65 feet (20 meters) or so but is the eventual loser. So if it can move better than a cheetah, is the car alive?

Moving down the list we have excretion. Everyone has a fair idea of this, and it is usually the wrong one. If we pictured someone excreting, we would probably subject ourselves to a rather disgusting image. However, we need not. Excretion is the removal of waste from inside the body. What we imagine to be excretion is defecation, which is the expulsion of unneeded food waste from the far end of the digestive system. From a topological point of view, where shapes are merely surfaces connected in a particular way, the gut is just as much on the outside of the body as the skin. From a functional point of view, it is a tube that begins at the mouth, twists and turns through the body, enlarging into various chambers along the way, and then finally reconnecting with the outside at the anus. Now imagine taking a two-dimensional slice of the body. Where is the tube now? It's gone, and in its place the body has been split in two.

> " Any unwanted or indigestible materials just carry on and leave through the rear opening. "

So the food that we swallow does not really go inside the body. However, it does pass through the middle of it, being digested and steadily broken down into simpler, more useful constituent parts. The nutrients in the gut are in the perfect place to be absorbed into the body proper. Any unwanted or indigestible materials just carry on and leave through the rear opening. The material that is expelled has never been inside the body, and so is not being excreted.

To illustrate this further, we can compare our situation with that of a placozoa. This is a simple type of animal. It is hard to think of one that is simpler. A placozoa is a tiny patch of cells that shuffles around on rocks on the seabed. It absorbs nutrients directly through its skin, eating bacteria and whatever else it slides across. That is not really any different from how we consume food. The only significant difference between us and a placozoa is that our body has a hole running through it like a doughnut. For want of a hole, the placozoa has been destined to stay a slimy patch of cells, while our hole, enlarged into a tube, has afforded us and most of the animal kingdom much broader horizons.

So both we and the placozoa have taken in nutrient substances—sugars, fats, etc.,—into the body. We may repurpose them to build and maintain the body itself, or we burn them to release the energy that fuels the other processes (more about this soon). Both the building and burning create waste, the former in the form of nitrogen-containing compounds left over from handling protein building blocks; the latter produces carbon dioxide and water.

> A placozoa is a tiny patch of cells that shuffles around on rocks on the seabed.

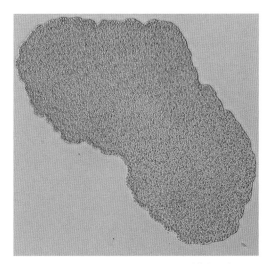

A living placozoa

We breathe out the carbon dioxide—this is true excretion. The placozoa just pushes it out through the skin. As for the nitrogen waste, humans convert it into a less toxic form called urea and get rid of it as a liquid waste—or urine. We also get rid of unwanted water this way. To save water (and reduce weight), birds and lizards excrete a solid form of nitrogen waste called uric acid. That is the white stuff in the droppings. Fish have no need to conserve water, and they excrete ammonia, a much more toxic form of nitrogen waste, but one that is safe enough when watered down.

I've been a little disingenuous so far. The brown coloring of the feces is actually supplied by an excretory process. The iron-rich hemoglobin in the old red blood cells is converted into a brown pigment, which is shed through the lining of the colon.

What about plants? Plants have a different relationship with nitrogen compounds and so do not need to excrete it. However, they do give out carbon dioxide during the night. During the day they are giving out oxygen, which is the waste product of photosynthesis. When we breathe in, we are taking in a deep gulp of plant excreta!

> "To save water (and reduce weight), birds and lizards excrete a solid form of nitrogen waste called uric acid."

So animals and plants are all excreting in their own way. What about the car? It excretes as well, pumping out waste gases from its exhaust. This car is looking more alive by the minute.

The car is also capable of the the next criterion of life: respiration. As with excretion, there is another misconception about this one as well. The word respiration is often used to mean the breathing process. Not every animal breathes, and plants don't, but they are alive nevertheless. They all respire after all.

The most correct meaning of the word "respiration" refers to a chemical process that takes place in every living cell. In the simplest terms, respiration is the combustion of sugar, releasing the energy needed to power all the other processes of life. It could be written like this:

$$C_6H_{12}O_6 + 6O_2 \rightarrow 6CO_2 + 6H_2O + energy$$

Is this an example of excretion?

Translating that into a more universal tongue, it says that a glucose molecule will react with six oxygen molecules to produce six carbon dioxides and six waters—plus some energy. This is a gross simplification of respiration. If this reaction were to take place all at once, all living things would explode in an instant. The actual process is a lot more convoluted, involving several steps that release the energy in smaller, more manageable amounts. In the 1930s, the entire process was figured out, most notably by Hans Krebs. The "Krebs Cycle," as it is sometimes called, is used by all aerobes, the organisms that use oxygen to burn their fuel. There are other ways of doing it: the bacteria in a bog and Usain Bolt sprinting in the 100m final are burning their fuels anaerobically, for a short time—at least

Who needs oxygen?

"The "Krebs Cycle," as it is sometimes called, is used by all aerobes, the organisms that use oxygen to burn their fuel. "

in Bolt's case. In the bog bacteria, that results in a stench of chemicals; Mr. Bolt may also do this occasionally, but in our illustration the anaerobic respiration produces lactic acids that build up in his muscles, creating the burn of fatigue. The oxygen from some deep breaths after the race will burn that all away again.

Back to aerobic respiration, the carbon dioxide and water are excreted. Animals gather the fuels they need by eating food; plants do it through photosynthesis, harnessing the energy in sunlight to make glucose. A car does not burn glucose, but it does use something similar. Glucose is a hexose, a sugar with six carbon atoms. Gasoline is chiefly octane, a chemical with eight carbon atoms in each molecule. So the car moves, excretes, and respires. But surely the next test will beat it.

> " Something that is alive must be able to make a copy of itself, or at least create a similar version. "

The second *R* in merring stands for reproduction. Something that is alive must be able to make a copy of itself, or at least create a similar version. And right away we can see that a car cannot reproduce itself. As if we didn't already know, a car is not alive.

In some ways, reproduction is the cause of death. There are many ways of doing it, but they all require a diversion of time, energy, and opportunity away from the main job of fueling and running the body. However, without reproduction, without at least attempting to produce another version of itself, an organism soon runs out of reasons to be alive. This fundamental drive is at the heart of the process of evolution by natural selection, where the fit survive and breed and the unfit do not.

Natural selection has led to a range of reproductive strategies, some that ensure a long life and others that do the opposite. The biology experts call the two basic versions "r-selection" and "K-selection." The capital K is important; it stands for "Kapazität," the German word for "capacity," and all German nouns are capitalized. The r stands for "rate."

If you were wondering, you were created by a K-selective strategy—perhaps by the most extreme example. Put simply, in K-selection, parents produce small numbers of offspring and devote large amounts of time and energy to raising them, teaching them, and keeping them safe. A human offspring is dependent on the parent until well into its teens— many readers might attest that in fact dependence lasts many years longer than that. However, the fundaments of biology get confused in the cultural and intellectual goings on of human society, so let's take a step back into the wild.

> " An orangutan baby lives with its mother— and is even suckled all this time—for seven years. "

The orangutan is said to have the longest childhood of any animal. Although whales, elephants, tigers, etc., take longer to grow to maturity due to their sheer size, orangutans are devoted parents—well mothers, anyway. The fathers have little to do with it.

An orangutan baby lives with its mother—and is even suckled all this time—for seven years. That is how long it takes for an orangutan to learn not just how to climb through the forest trees safely but also how to identify the best food, learn where to find it season by season, how to build nests to rest in, and how to handle other orangutans.

An orangutan mother has only one baby at a time (twins are, of course, a possibility), and there is an eight-year gap between births. This is where the K for Kapazität comes in. K-selective strategies have a birth rate that aims to keep the local population at full capacity—the precise number of individuals depends on the local habitat. So it is normal for the average female fertility to be two, which means every female has two babies, and the population size stays constant from generation to generation.

> " While an orangutan has a baby once every eight years, an oceanic sunfish pumps out 300 million eggs in one go. "

The r-selective strategy aims to push the limit—and push it to mass destruction. While an orangutan has a baby once every eight years, an oceanic sunfish pumps out 300 million eggs in one go. For some background the oceanic sunfish is the largest bony fish in the sea—it literally weighs a metric ton—and has a habit of sunbathing near the surface, hence the name.

Orangutans and oceanic sunfish employ vastly different reproductive strategies.

With every female fish producing such an amazing quantity of eggs, one might expect that the world's oceans are teeming with these giant fish. A quick inspection from the coast does not confirm this hypothesis, and nor do reports from ocean-going vessels, which would have to cut their way through the crowds of sunfish.

In fact, sunfish are quite rare. The carrying capacity of the oceans—the number of sunfish the sea can hold—is far lower than 300 million. So every single female sunfish is producing more eggs than the entire global population of the species.

Something's not adding up somewhere. Firstly, not all the eggs are fertilized. These fish use external fertilization, so as the females are pumping out eggs at the breeding grounds, males are pumping out clouds of sperm to mingle with them, and perhaps fertilize a few million.

A fertilized sunfish egg will develop into a fry barely .07 inches (2 mm) across. To make it to adulthood, it needs to expand in size 60 million times over. The number of eggs among that original 300 million,

> A fertilized sunfish egg will develop into a fry barely 0.07 inches (2 mm) across.

which make the full journey to fully grown adult is tiny, a fraction of a fraction of a percent. Perhaps just one or two.

As we've seen the *r* in r-selective stands for "rate," and sunfish are focused on the rate of reproduction not the capacity of the habitat. They are simply playing the odds. If one fish can produce twice as many eggs as their neighbor along the reef, then they will have twice as many offspring that reach breeding age themselves. That kind of competition for quantity not quality has led to the mind-boggling numbers of eggs and the seemingly huge waste of r-selection. However, despite the huge energy required to make so many eggs and the fact that roughly 99.99 percent of them will die within hours if not days, sunfish can be pretty certain that their reproductive attempts are successful. The orangutan meanwhile is putting all of its hopes in two maybe three children throughout a normal lifespan. Despite all that care and attention, a tree 130 feet (40 m) above the ground is not an entirely safe place to raise a baby.

Life is all about these kinds of trade offs.

> " Perhaps its speed is varied according to external factors, such as the supply of components and the demand for robots on other production lines? "

Are robots alive?

The car's lack of breeding potential has seen it transferred to the inanimate pile, but we can imagine machines that are still alive and kicking according to the four criteria covered so far. Cars are made by robots, not entirely of course, but let's say for the sake of argument that they are. It does not take much more of an argument to imagine a production line of robots that manufacture production-line robots. This is reproduction in the loosest sense. Is such a robot r-selective or K-selective? It would depend on how fast the production line is running. Perhaps its speed is varied according to external factors, such as the supply of components and the demand for robots on other production lines? If this were the case, our imaginary robot has already passed the fifth test of life.

> " The human body is bristling with sensors, quite literally. "

Number five is irritability. In a medical sense this word describes an overreaction to a stimulus. If you punched someone because they tickled your foot, bystanders might describe you as being somewhat irritable. If you punched someone because they punched you, onlookers would take a different view. Either way, the police will probably need to be involved.

In the biological sense, irritability is a clumsy term. We needed an *i* for the acronym to work, remember. It is meant to describe how a living body is sensitive to and able to respond to its surroundings. Perhaps you are doing that now, feeling the thrill of knowledge … or stifling a yawn. (The former, I'm hoping, and will plow on with that in mind.)

The human body is bristling with sensors, quite literally. Your skin is capable of detecting heat, cold, and different levels of pressure—even tiny gusts of wind. The skin can respond in many ways to these stimuli—and may do several things at once. A nasty pinprick on the fingertip makes you recoil right away because of a motor (or muscle) response, and blood rushes to the wound and forms a temporary clot that seals it from the outside world. While the skin is being repaired, the fingertip will swell slightly. The amount of blood in the area has gone up to aid with the repair, and it is also there to ward off any invading germs that have snuck in through the wound. The swelling makes the fingertip tender, and it hurts if you fail to protect it while it heals. If you do not look after the sore finger, you will probably experience the literary irony of your irritability making you irritable!

Spiders, like humans, have responses based on the quality of irritability.

This is just one example of how a living body responds to its surroundings. Animals also use eyes, ears, noses, tongues, antennae, plus chemical, heat, and electrical sensors to collect

> " Plants are also able to respond to external conditions, just in a slower way. "

information from their surroundings. Plants are also able to respond to external conditions, just in a slower way. For example, anyone who has been clearing out an outhouse or cleaning up a patch of rough ground may remember seeing long pale plant stems growing under a rock, board, or other object that has blocked out the light.

What has happened is a seed has sprouted, and its stem is racing toward the light. This initial growth spurt is fueled by the oils and proteins packed away in the seed and embryonic leaves, but the plant needs to get to the light quickly. It

grows by cell division (like all life—more on that later), but individual cells can also lengthen to help with the search for light. In the dark of the soil (where most seeds start out), the cells lengthen under the influence of a light-sensitive hormone, known as an auxin. Light inhibits auxin, and so in the dark, the stem grows long and straight. Once it hits the light, this form of growth slows down.

> Once it hits the light, this form of growth slows down.

The system still has a role to play, however. Light does not fall on the plant evenly, and so the effect of the auxin is stronger on the shaded side than the illuminated side. The cells on the darker side grow longer, and the result is the stem bending toward the light. Now the plant is illuminated all over, maximizing its growing potential. This ubiquitous plant behavior shows that it is not just animals that respond to the surroundings.

Plants respond to light.

Johnson High School Library, Buda TX

We are on the home straight now: nutrition is the next test. We have touched on this subject already, and we will address how living things acquire their nutrition in a later chapter. For now, all that is required is to say that a living thing needs a supply of raw materials, most often boiled down to three

> 66 Simple carbohydrates are sugars
>   like glucose and sucrose.   99

major groups: carbohydrates, proteins, and fats. As their name suggests, carbohydrates are substances made from water and carbon (hydrated carbons, to be exact). Simple carbohydrates are sugars like glucose and sucrose. They can be chained together to make complex carbohydrates such as starch and cellulose. The simple carbohydrates are used chiefly as fuel, packets of chemical energy that can be put to work making and breaking other chemicals in the cell. Starch is a store of energy, forming a concentrated blob that can be packed away and then broken up into simpler sugars when needed. Cellulose, in contrast, is a structural element. It is the stuff used to surround the cells of plants and give plants as a whole some rigidity.

Plants make all the carbohydrates they need by photosynthesis, and animals just eat plants (or an animal that has eaten plants) to get hold of it. Animals can make use of starch in much the same way as a plant, but the cellulose is largely indigestible. (It's what is listed as fiber on food packaging.)

Nutrition in pictures

A better term than fat is lipid—a solid lipid is a fat, while a liquid one is an oil. Lipids have structural roles in the body. The diaphanous membranes that surround all cells are made from ingenious films of lipid. Animals may also use fats as a long-term store of energy. It is more calorific than sugar (it releases more energy) but is harder to handle.

> 66 Animal fats tend to be solid and this is due to one simple difference in their chemistry compared to the oily lipids of a plant. 99

Animal fats tend to be solid and this is due to one simple difference in their chemistry compared to the oily lipids of a plant. You may be aware that one is saturated and the other is unsaturated. To understand what that means, we need a quick look at the structure of a lipid. Put simply, a lipid is a chemical jellyfish, with a head molecule trailing three long acids made up of chains of carbon atoms. The carbon atoms can be bonded to each other or to hydrogens. A saturated fat is saturated with hydrogens. In an unsaturated one, the carbon chains have only a few hydrogens. The hydrogens make the chains cling together and tangle with those of neighboring lipids. The result of that is the saturated fats are cloying, waxy solids, while the unsaturated fats are runny oils. A quick aside here: the butter substitute margarine is famously made from unsaturated plant fats. However, it is converted from an oil to a spreadable solid by bubbling hydrogen through it. It's actually little more involved than that, but the upshot is the unsaturated fat becomes an artificial version of saturated fat. I'll leave the reader to wonder why one would bother to do that.

Finally, we come to the proteins. Each protein is a construction of thousands of smaller molecules called amino acids. These are Lego bricks of life. There are about twenty different amino acids used by the living world, but together they can be arranged in myriad combinations, each producing a protein with a unique set of characteristics. Protein structures are mind-bogglingly complex: the primary structure is a main chain of amino acids, but that begins to fold in on itself creating an intricate tangle, the precise shape of which depends on the original order of acids.

So there is a lot more to a protein than a slab of rump steak. Proteins are the tools used by life processes. The shape of muscle proteins allows them to create the forces and movements in your body. All enzymes are proteins. Their shape is a perfect fit for their job. They latch onto or engulf other chemicals to split, modify, or combine them into new materials as needed. Every protein used in the body is coded for in the genes, written down in the DNA (short for deoxyribonucleic acid). Does this mean that life, in the end, is just a very big chemical reaction?

> The shape of muscle proteins allows them to create the forces and movements in your body.

The main purpose of nutrition is growth, the final test of life. All multicellular organisms—you, me, the placozoa, and the tree that was once this page—grew from a single initial cell. We developed according to a plan. Some plans, when they began, were very similar, but pretty soon, we developed in our separate ways. Even, eventually, you and I.

The purpose of growth is to achieve a state suitable for reproduction. The placozoa need not develop very much—it can simply break off a piece of its body and call it "son." But what of single-celled organisms? They reproduce by splitting in two. For them, what is the difference between growth and reproduction? The answer is not a lot, but if we look for it we can find a distinction: sex.

> " The placozoa need not develop very much—it can simply break off a piece of its body and call it "son." "

Even the smallest bacteria engages in sexual reproduction. They may be able to "grow" in number by simply splitting in two, but they can also make new individuals by mixing their DNA. The products of this sexual activity is not the "growth" of the original parent but the formation of a new, unique individual.

THE
BIG ANSWER

So we have wandered far and wide over the subject, but have we gotten any closer to an answer? Let's try to reduce the nature of life to its simplest form. In 2000, a new set of criteria for life was proposed. An acronym is no use here; there are only two: 1) life needs a self-replicating molecule and 2) it must be capable of performing at least one thermodynamic work cycle.

> " A thermodynamic work cycle is a process where energy of one type is converted into another form and made to do some work. "

The first rule is easy enough to confirm. All our cells have DNA. They also have RNA, which is a related molecule used to translate the DNA code into proteins. Scientists suggest that RNA (ribonucleic acid) is more ancient than DNA and a little more robust. A flask of RNA mixed in with its constituent building blocks—the sugar ribose, some phosphates, and a few acids—will replicate itself. It uses its own molecules as a template for its daughters. So something as "simple" as RNA (it's actually a very complex molecule) can pass the first test on its own.

Now for number two. A thermodynamic work cycle is a process where energy of one type is converted into another form and made to do some work. By work we mean break something, make something, or move something. Work in this context comes from the world of physics. Engineers have been making machines that do work for centuries. In fact, the first machine was the hand axe, which, at more than a million years old, predates humanity itself. However, only the biological realm can combine the machine aspect—the cell and the body at large are machines, just like some pliers or a combine harvester—with the molecular replication. So in the end, life requires a machine that is able to copy and then read (but not comprehend) its design blueprint.

At this point, our thought experiment with an almost-alive robot-making robot has reached its breaking point. We can continue to imagine a robot that apes a biological body with a mechanical one. We can imagine that it can regulate its own processes, source its own fuel and the raw materials it needs, and build copies of itself, perhaps even designing new variations with tweaks to its blueprints. This is science fiction, of course, and sci-fi often renders such living machines as giant, piston-actuated, gas-guzzling metallic monsters covered in wires. The question is whether the technologies we use today—computers and engines, etc.—are up to the challenge of life? Or if we are to build artificial lifeforms, will they have bodies made from metals, plastics, and other inanimate materials? Or will they be using the same biological substances that make up our own physiology? And if so, does that mean they are still artificial?

> " The main purpose of nutrition is growth, the final test of life. "

The future or a vision from the past?

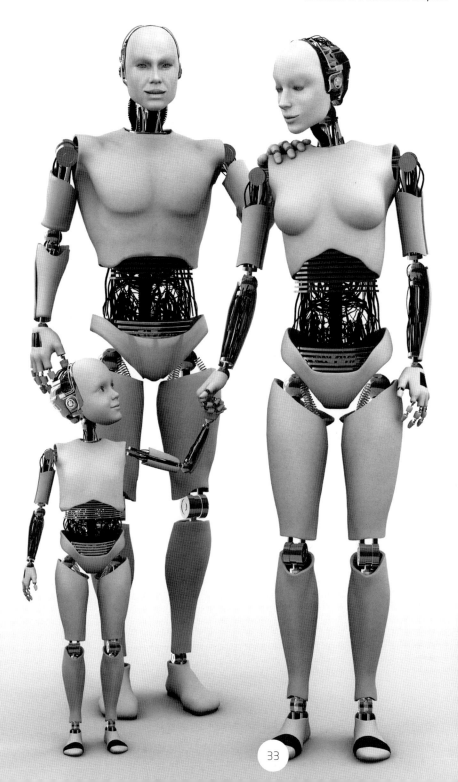

Q2

IS THERE **MORE** THAN **ONE WAY** OF **BEING ALIVE?**

A cursory look at the wonders of the natural world, the wealth of species estimated to number anywhere from three to thirty million, might make this appear like a simple question with a simple answer. Each one of those species occupies a unique niche in its habitat. It has evolved to live in a particular way, to exploit a particular set of resources, and coexist with a particular set of neighboring species. Each species is one moving part in the machine that is the global ecosystem. So the answer is that there are millions of ways of being alive— although the exact number of millions is open to question.

> There are just two ways of being alive—and two distinct avenues toward death. Life scientists divide life into autotrophs and heterotrophs.

You could also answer the question a different way. There are just two ways of being alive—and two distinct avenues toward death. Life scientists divide life into autotrophs and heterotrophs. The distinction comes from the way organisms obtain the energy that powers their lives. All becomes clearer when we pick apart the terminology. The term "-troph" comes from the Greek for something like "feeder" or "eater." Autotrophs therefore are "self eaters," while heterotrophs are "other eaters." In case you were wondering, you are a heterotroph. That means you obtain your energy by consuming the chemicals stored inside another life form—or at the very least extracted from a once-living organism.

The autotrophs count plants among their number, single-celled plant-like organisms called algae, and many types of bacteria. (The most abundant organism on Earth is a bacterium called Prochlorococcus that lives in the oceans. Biologists predict that are three octillion of them!)

Heterotrophs include animals; fungi; a wealth of single-celled bugs called things like amoeba, ciliates, or protozoa; plus the rest of the bacteria.

This all relates to the first *R* in MERRING, the acronym of life. *R* stands for "respiration," which is the process by which organisms extract energy from chemical fuel. The process is long and involved, but it is essentially an example of oxidation. Combustion, or burning, is also an oxidation, and the outcome of both processes is essentially the same.

" The word "oxidation" implies that a chemical is being altered by the addition of oxygen during some kind of reaction. "

A heterotroph meets an autotroph.

Glucose is the primary fuel of life.

There are several fuels used by life but to simplify things we will just use the simplest one: glucose. The word "oxidation" implies that a chemical is being altered by the addition of oxygen during some kind of reaction. That is not wrong, although oxidations can occur that do not use oxygen. Put simply (or perhaps not), something is oxidized if it loses electrons during a reaction.

As we have already seen, glucose is oxidized into carbon dioxide and water by respiration. That releases energy, which powers all life. In the case of we heterotrophs, our focus is simply to secure and consume glucose (or nutritious chemicals like it). Then we oxidize it and move on to get some more. This activity encompasses everything from an amoeba engulfing a bacterium and a fungus oozing digestive juices into its surroundings and absorbing the nutrients released from dead and decaying matter, to booking a table at your favorite restaurant.

    The apex predators—sharks and tigers etc.—only eat other heterotrophs, gleaning all their nutrients from the flesh of animals.

Since we are heterotrophs and rather important ones, we imagine ourselves at or near the top of a **trophic pyramid**. More on why this should be a pyramid later, but essentially heterotrophs operate in a hierarchy. The apex predators—sharks and tigers etc.—only eat other heterotrophs, gleaning all their nutrients from the flesh of animals. Hanging around in the middle are the omnivores. If it were not for our domination of natural food webs, we humans would be firmly in this category. Omnivores eat a bit of everything, both heterotrophs and autotrophs. Of course, most animals eat only autotrophs. We call them herbivores, or primary consumers.

However, the sharp-eyed among you will have spotted something. All the nutrients are coming from the autotrophs, the plants. In terms of food chains, autotrophs are called primary producers. They form the base of the trophic pyramid, the foundation upon which the rest of life is built.

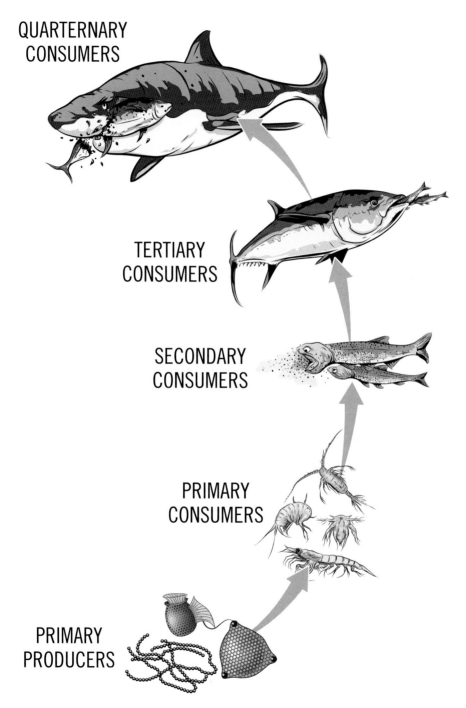

QUARTERNARY
CONSUMERS

TERTIARY
CONSUMERS

SECONDARY
CONSUMERS

PRIMARY
CONSUMERS

PRIMARY
PRODUCERS

Heterotrophs have the starring role in food chains. But it all begins with the autotrophs.

Leaves using their powers of reduction

So what are they doing differently? As well as being able to oxidize glucose during respiration, autotrophs are capable of doing the opposite, a process known as reduction. For every oxidation, there is always a reduction. As with the term oxidation, reduction needs some explaining. The word is derived from smelting, where ore is "reduced" to its pure metallic form. In this case, what is happening is that the oxygen in the ore is being removed during the smelting reaction. Specifically, it is reacting with carbon and carbon monoxide to form carbon dioxide. The carbon is being oxidized by the ore, and the ore is being reduced by the carbon.

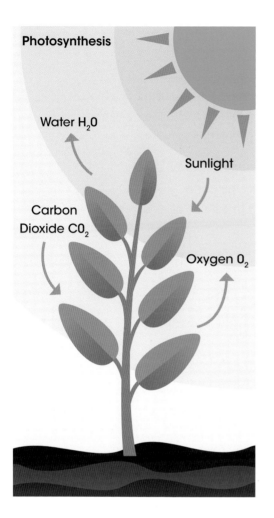

Photosynthesis

Water H$_2$0

Sunlight

Carbon
Dioxide C0$_2$

Oxygen 0$_2$

So what does an autotroph reduce?

By far, the most common form of autotrophy is photosynthesis. This is the process where an organism captures the energy in light and uses it to make, or synthesize, glucose—the term means "making with light." The photosynthesis reaction is the opposite of the respiration one. So while the latter oxidizes glucose to make carbon dioxide, the former reduces carbon dioxide to make glucose (at least the raw materials for it).

The metabolic pathways that enable this miraculous reaction are not simply the ones used in respiration run in reverse. Far from it, they are an entirely different animal—or more pertinently they are not animal at all! Photosynthesis makes it possible for plants to convert the energy in the sun's light into chemical energy packed away inside glucose. Its raw ingredients are the gas carbon dioxide, which it takes from the air (or water) whenever it needs it; and water, which it collects from the soil (or its surroundings in general).

There is great fanfare given to chlorophyll, the green pigment that traps the energy in sunlight ready for use in photosynthesis. However, the workhorse of the operation is another chemical called rubisco, short for ribulose-1,5-bisphosphate carboxylase/oxygenase, which begins to build the glucose out of carbon dioxide taken from the air.

The intended purpose of the glucose is to power plants survival and reproduction. However, the entire animal and fungal kingdoms have been able to make use of it, as well.

> " There is great fanfare given to chlorophyll, the green pigment that traps the energy in sunlight ready for use in photosynthesis. "

Photosynthesis is not the only player in town, however, and was probably a late arrival among the autotrophic community. Other autotrophs are chemosynthetic, which means they get the energy they need to build their nutrients using inorganic substances. While photosynthesis can reduce carbon dioxide, it is also oxidizing water, which cleaves the molecule in two to make oxygen and hydrogen. The oxygen—fortunately for us—is a waste product and is discarded. What the continuing process uses is the highly energized hydrogens that can be used to build the complex, energy-rich glucose compounds.

Home sweet home for a chemosynthetic organism

Chemosynthetic organisms need hydrogen as well but get it in a different way. They live in chemical soup habitats, such as volcanic pools and vents, or even inside rocks, where natural gases, such as methane or hydrogen sulphide are circulating from deep inside the planet.

43

▲ *Most photosynthesis takes place in the ocean …*

These gases take the place of water in photosynthesis and are oxidized to release the useful hydrogen. In the case of hydrogen sulphide, which is the most common chemosynthesis ingredient, the waste product is sulphur, not oxygen. Unlike oxygen, sulphur is a solid and cannot be left to waft away. Instead the chemosynthetic organisms, which are almost exclusively bacteria (or ancient cousins of bacteria) known as archaea, have to store this waste sulphur in their cell bodies. That simple—almost innocuous—difference between starting points is enough to make the difference between organisms that grow ten stories high and teem in their multiple billions in the oceans and organisms restricted to life as a single cell.

> "These gases take the place of water in photosynthesis and are oxidized to release the useful hydrogen."

… Although most plants live on land. ▶

THE
BIG ANSWER

As we have seen, there are two major divisions between lifeforms: the self-reliant autotrophs and the heterotrophs that take advantage of their largesse. (We should mention that some single-celled organisms are able to behave as autotrophs and heterotrophs simultaneously, like minute triffids fueled by the sun but also by gorging on flesh.)

While autotrophs appear to have life figured out— they can do it all themselves with the simplest of raw materials—they are more limited in where they can live. The dark oceans are the largest habitat on the planet, but photosynthetic creatures can never venture there. It is just too dark. The heterotrophs go wherever there is food to be had.

> " The heterotrophs go wherever there is food to be had. "

The exotic chemical soup consumed by the chemotrophs is not that available, at the surface at least. The awesome power of the oxygen released by plants has altered the chemistry of the air and water at the surface so much that those chemotrophic conditions are a rarity. It is difficult to look, but it is possible that unimaginably immense armies of chemotrophs are living in the rocks deep under foot.

The fundamental division between life forms is based on chemistry and harnessing free energy to the aims of life. Those aims appear to run contrary to the overall rules of the universe, which is destined to cool down and become more spread out and chaotic. How is it that life can create such order?

Q3

DOES LIFE BREAK THE **LAWS** OF **PHYSICS?**

The study of life and death dominates science through the many branches of medical research and biology, its more outdoorsy cousin. Some people go further and wrap life science into a general love of nature. To nature lovers, to all of us, really, living things have a special, privileged, perhaps even sacred place in the great scheme of things. Few argue that life does not warrant this kind of attitude, but with it comes a view that life is ruled by some special, possibly supernatural force that lies outside of the normal laws of the universe. In particular, the laws of thermodynamics are frequently pointed to as not applying to life. Could this be true?

The universe is a one-way street—there is no possibility of going back. We can best understand this as time. We and everything in the universe are moving through time. We may do it at different speeds (don't ask!), but we are always going in the same direction, from the past to the future, via the present.

66 The universe is a one-way street—there is no possibility of going back. 99

Time is passing.

We are all aware of "the arrow of time," the sun rises and sets each dawn and dusk, the seasons roll around year after year, and we are well aware that our lives occupy a limited segment on the timeline. We are born, we live, and, in time, we will die.

The thing is nobody really knows what the time is. If you find out, perhaps you could note it down for us—but it won't stay correct for long. In the next instant, the time has moved on.

> " The past and the future exist only in our memories and imaginations. "

Philosophers have had a go at telling the time. They propose three possible ways that time works. Firstly, time is made up of future events, present events, and past events. As you might have already surmised, future events always become present events and then past events. It is not possible for past events to become present or future ones. The second idea is a tweak of the first: it is possible to order objects according to whether they existed earlier or later to each other. In both concepts, past objects, which existed a long time ago, are just as real as the ones that exist right now. It is possible that future objects already exist, but we'll just have to wait and see about those. There is a third idea that says that the only things that exist do so in the present. Every step forward in time destroys whatever caused it to happen and will be destroyed by any effect it results in. Because we cannot observe the past or future, this final "presentist" theory is the best fit for our experience of time. The past and the future exist only in our memories and imaginations.

Time can be measured, though. You are well aware of that every time you are running later for an appointment. When all is said and done, the tick tock of the universe is the steady increase in something called entropy. Entropy is a measure of the disorder of matter. It is inextricably tied up with the transfer of energy. According to laws of thermodynamics, the energy of a discrete system will always go down, while the entropy will always increase.

It takes energy to hold matter together, and as time's arrow flies, that energy is spreading out from where it is concentrated to where it is not. The matter that once held the energy is gradually breaking apart into a more and more disordered state. This is the rule behind the familiar idea that heat always flows from hot objects to colder objects, never the other way around.

Whether it is a wind-up clockwork wristwatch or the latest nuclear clock, all timepieces are given some energy and they dissipate it in a regular fashion, counting out the inexorable rise in entropy as the universe steadily uncoils.

> " When all is said and done, the tick tock of the universe is the steady increase in something called entropy. "

The flow of energy is what is making heat and light stream out of the sun, warming our planet as it rolls around its orbit. That source of energy is what supports life on Earth—or at least most of it. The light is captured by autotrophic plants and algae and converted into the tasty foods for us heterotrophs. (Even the chemicals devoured by the rock-eating chemotrophs were made by a sun, albeit a long-dead one from a previous generation that made those elements during its final few billion years of life.)

Energy arriving ▶

However, on Earth at least, the natural order of things seems to be turned back to front. The stream of energy is used by life to create order not disorder. The entropy of a glucose molecule is lower than that of its ingredients. In turn, the energy released from the glucose during respiration is used to create more and more complex and ordered structures. They say we go from dust to dust, but in between we are the most intricately ordered objects in the known universe.

> 66 Life processes are just another of the many phenomena that are possible in the universe. 99

Could it be that life follows a different set of rules to the rest of the dead, cooling universe? Some see this apparent effect as evidence that life is governed by some supernatural vital power, beyond the scope of science. Others take a different view. Life processes are just another of the many phenomena that are possible in the universe. Can life really trump the laws of physics? Whatever the answer, one thing is certain: life is truly remarkable.

THE
BIG ANSWER

This question could be answered very quickly: no. Nothing can break the laws of physics. If they could, we would just have to change the laws of physics to match them. Physics, as the foundation of science, seeks to find the rules that underlie the way the universe works—everything in the universe, including that oh-so-special case, life.

> " Thermodynamics frequently makes reference to the action of closed systems. "

However, there is no need to rewrite the laws of physics to understand the way life handles energy. Thermodynamics frequently makes reference to the action of closed systems. That means there is no energy coming in or leaving. An engine that has its supply of fuel cut off becomes a closed system. It will eventually—pretty quickly, in fact—stop working as its supply of energy becomes unavailable to its moving parts. A living body does the same when it becomes too disordered to harness its energy.

Energy cannot be created from nothing, nor can it be destroyed. The quantity of energy in the universe has remained constant since the big bang. What has happened in the intervening years is that the energy has been converted from one form to another. That is all that a machine is doing, whether a mechanical one or biological one like a living body.

What kinds of energy are there? Sound, heat, light, motion, electricity, and more are all are all kinds of energy. A machine takes a supply of one and converts it into another, or at least alters the way that energy acts. A lever is a simple machine that converts the energy of a downward motion into an upward motion. A wheel converts a linear motion into a rotational one. An engine converts the heat energy from a burning fuel into a motion of some mechanical parts. A plant is a machine that converts light energy into the chemical energy of a sugar molecule.

A potential perpetual motion machine

Everyone who has cycled up a hill or felt the heat of their car hood at the end of a long journey will testify that no energy conversion, not even in natural processes, is 100 percent efficient. Many have imagined the wonders of technology if energy could be used with perfect efficiency. Their goal was a perpetual motion machine, a device where the energy of its motion was captured and recycled so it kept on moving in perpetuity. Several designs for perpetual motion machines have survived the ages. If any were built, they proved to be found wanting—although some charlatans managed to pass off their constructions as the real deal.

The problem was the pesky laws of thermodynamics. At every stage, some of the energy was lost as heat, staying in the closed system but becoming useless. For the machine to carry on working, useful energy had be in constant supply from outside the system.

The same thing is happening in metabolic processes. Photosynthesis, that marvel of biochemistry, is only about 6 percent efficient! A big inefficiency is the green color of the leaves. This is due to the green (and yellow) light from the sun being reflected by the chlorophylls inside. They absorb only the blue and red stuff. If chlorophyll was able to make use of all light from the sun, then plants would have black leaves.

> " Their goal was a perpetual motion machine, a device where the energy of its motion was captured and recycled so it kept on moving in perpetuity. "

Every machination of a biological system results in heat energy being lost. Many organisms operate at an optimal temperature and devote entire body systems to maintaining it. We shed excess heat (by sweating, for example) and cling on to heat when it is cold outside. That's enough to give you goose bumps—that is from our thin covering of body hair being elevated to trap more warm air close to the skin.

So where are we when it comes to our question? Life on Earth is not a closed system. The ultimate source of its energy comes from the sun, and the heat of all that biological activity is eventually shed into outer space, radiating out into the emptiness. One day, infinitesimal traces of that heat might shine down on another planet harboring life. It won't add up to much at all, but it is possible.

On the planet-sized scale, the laws of thermodynamics are up and running perfectly. But what about looking at the problem one organism at a time? Let's move our thinking on from plants. A humble heterotroph, let's say a shrew, consumes its body weight in seeds every day. Does it convert all of those seeds into energy and replacement body parts? Definitely not, otherwise shrews would soon become giant creatures marauding through the landscape. Much of the energy content of the seed food is unavailable to the shrew, and what it does manage to extract is rapidly lost as heat.

> **One day, infinitesimal traces of that heat might shine down on another planet harboring life.**

A shrew battles entropy.

Tiny shrews have to eat even more than their body weight each day to survive. Larger animals can survive on smaller proportions of food because they lose heat more slowly, but the process is much the same.

The owls and foxes that survive by eating shrews do not eat anything near their body weight in food. However, there are far fewer of them around than their prey. Simplifying the complexity of food chains into an overall big picture provides the best evidence that thermodynamics are alive and well in the biological realm: the layers of organisms in the food chain form a pyramid. Those in the base layer are the primary producers, like plants and other photosynthetic organisms. Primary producers outweigh all the heterotrophs by 1,000 to 1. The next level up are the herbivores. As a rule of thumb, they are able to use about 10 percent of the total energy content they consume in their plant food. So for every metric ton of plants eaten, about 220 pounds (100 kg) of herbivore is sustained. The same rule works with the higher layers in the trophic pyramid. The secondary consumers (often omnivores like us) eat the herbivores. About 22 pounds (10 kg) of omnivore is sustained from that original metric ton of plants. At the apex of the pyramid are the apex predators—shark, lions, etc. Only 2.2 pounds (1 kg) of lion results from the original metric ton of plants.

> ❝ Much of the energy content of the seed food is unavailable to the shrew, and that which it does manage to extract is rapidly lost as heat. ❞

ENERGY PYRAMID

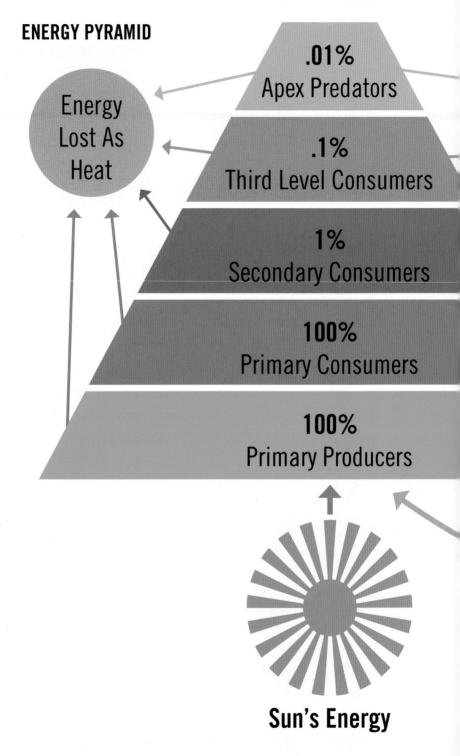

.01%
Apex Predators

.1%
Third Level Consumers

1%
Secondary Consumers

100%
Primary Consumers

100%
Primary Producers

Energy Lost As Heat

Sun's Energy

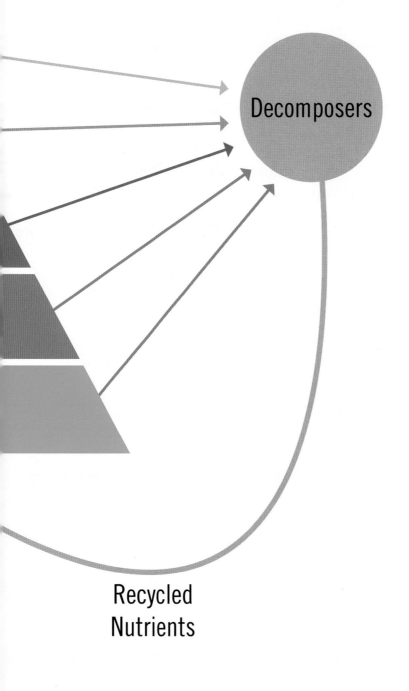

Decomposers

Recycled
Nutrients

The trophic pyramid

However, the trophic pyramid also shows that the energy content of food becomes more concentrated at each layer. While a cow has to eat literally tons of un-nutritious plant food each year to power its metabolism, meat eaters feast on more refined, energy-rich meals. Although the energy flow through the trophic layers does not contravene the laws of thermodynamics, life does still appear able to build order out of disorder. Is that something only life can do?

Well, only if you think your refrigerator is alive. A fridge is an example of a heat pump, which is a machine that is able to push energy in the opposite direction from the rest of the universe. A warm object will cool as its heat spreads to colder objects. The heat-pumping fridge does the opposite, it uses a source of energy to make heat leave a cold area—making it perpetually chilly. A living body is a natural heat pump in that it is pushing energy the wrong way, albeit for a short time. Mechanical heat pumps were developed over the last 250 years or so; life, the natural heat pump, has been doing it for a lot longer. But there is no special science behind it; both are making use of the same laws of physics.

66 Although the energy flow through the trophic layers does not contravene the laws of thermodynamics, life does still appear able to build order out of disorder. 99

A fridge is a heat pump—just like you.

Q4

HOW DID
LIFE
START?

The ways and means through which life can exist are well understood, each able to harness some kind of energy to its own ends. How on earth—or anywhere else—could such a complex system have arisen?

The ways and means through which life can exist are well understood, each able to harness some kind of energy to its own ends. How on earth—or anywhere else—could such a complex system have arisen? As we have seen, life science is an arm, albeit a very large and powerful one—of chemistry and physics. It can be understood as a flow of energy and through a series of self-regulating chemical reactions. It is possible, therefore, to plot a hypothetical path from simple nonliving chemicals to complex chemical structures that begin to show the attributes of life.

The precise route of that path remains open to a fascinating debate with alternatives taking in many points of interests along the way from the primordial soup, deep sea vents, hot rocks, and even outer space. Until comparatively recently, however, the very idea that life arose from purely physical nature was regarded as ridiculous. The prevailing view was that the process of life must be driven by some "vital" force that was distinct from biology and not seen in the more base sciences.

> 66 The prevailing view was that the process of life must be driven by some "vital" force that was distinct from biology and not seen in the more base sciences. 99

Galen

This idea stemmed from the founders of medical science, such as Greco-Roman medic Galen from the second century CE. He assumed that the brute anatomy of a body was not enough to sustain life. Instead a spark—divine or otherwise—of vitality was needed to get it all working. In the 1780s, the Italian physician Luigi Galvani thought he had managed to tap this vital spark when he succeeded in generating electric currents in the freshly removed legs of a dead frog—and after much macabre experimentation—the corpses of all kinds of animals. This discovery of "animal electricity" was momentous. It paved the way for

Luigi Galvani

batteries, circuitry, and, in the end, the electronics—plus the investigation of the electrical activity of the body helped us to understand the workings of the nervous system and the brain. However, was a special vital force really required for life?

> The reasoning was that chemistry could not wrangle the vital force. Only life could synthesize organic molecules.

A simple accident in a chemistry lab in the 1820s snuffed out the concept of "vital force." Until then, chemists drew a distinction between the "organic" molecules that were found inside bodies— and the stuff derived from it—and the "inorganic" compounds that made up the rest of the stuff of nature. The organic chemicals had so far defied the tools of chemistry. When they were exposed to conditions outside the the limited range of life—for example when heated in the laboratory—they became "denatured," buckling into lifeless, inorganic forms. The reasoning was that chemistry could not wrangle the vital force. Only life could synthesize organic molecules.

In 1828, Freidrich Wöhler, a German chemist, decided to see if he could make ammonium cyanate. This is a chemical linked to the deadly poison cyanide. It is made up of nitrogen, carbon, hydrogen, and oxygen. Wöhler had some success in making this stuff, but he found that his store of the chemical became contaminated with urea.

Freidrich Wöhler

Urea is the chemical that gives urine its name. It is a toxic waste product from the metabolism of proteins. That process yields nitrogen compounds that are unhelpful to the body and must be removed. This is one of the chief functions of excretion. Wöhler's inorganic cyanate was spontaneously reforming itself into organic urea. Had his apparatus come alive in some way? Obviously not. The barrier between organic and inorganic substances was a false one—even the chemicals of life obeyed the same set of rules as everything else.

> It had just appeared, either by a divine hand or by spontaneous generation.

If that were the case, then there was no need for a vital force to make life possible. Chemistry could do it. One of the fathers of modern chemistry, Antoine Lavoisier, had already demonstrated that animal bodies took in oxygen and gave out carbon dioxide—just like the way a burning log consumed oxygen from the air and produced carbon dioxide. Simple chemistry it is not, but the body is "burning" fuel for energy in the same kind of way.

Antoine Lavoisier analyzing breath

These discoveries demystified life, making it something that scientists could investigate in the same way that they might study the weather or rocks. However, the origin of life remained a big mystery. Although the vital force faded from scientists' theories, other age-old ideas were still the ones used to tackle the problem.

Since ancient times, both religion and natural philosophy had offered the same answer to how life had originated: it had just appeared, either by a divine hand or by spontaneous generation.

> " In the late seventeenth century, the newly invented microscope had begun to broaden the horizons of biology. "

Every parent would testify that their children did not appear spontaneously, and the same could be said for any large animal. By "large," we mean anything complex enough to be seen without a microscope. These big organisms were formed by **biogenesis**. In other words, their life could only have come from other life. This is true enough but of no help in understanding where and how the first life arose.

In the late seventeenth century, the newly invented microscope had begun to broaden the horizons of biology. Researchers saw tiny creatures, or "animalcules," through their eyepieces. These are now better known as amoeba and protozoa (among other things) and bacteria—once the power of microscopes was up to the job of seeing these smallest of life forms.

The best place to see microorganisms was in fetid liquids and putrid foods—or other dead remains. The prevailing theory at the dawn of the 1800s was that biogenesis did not apply to the tiny organisms. Instead, theorists said they arose spontaneously from the chemicals left over by life, a process that was named abiogenesis.

These were the days before Darwin and also before the great age of Earth was fully understood. So, in the context of a young planet with natural history going back centuries rather than eons, the idea that life arrived via the "spontaneous generation" of microorganisms seemed like a workable idea.

However, the list of organisms that appeared in this fashion was getting shorter. Researchers time and again traced the life cycles of different organisms, from fungus to bacteria, and showed that time and again they were biogenetic. In other words, even bacteria had parents.

In the 1860s, Darwin's theory of evolution by natural selection changed the playing field. According to his theory, all life on Earth has evolved from a string

> " In the 1860s, Darwin's theory of evolution by natural selection changed the playing field. "

of ancestors taking us all back to a single common ancestor that lived long ago—we now know that was at least three billion years in the past. Darwin explained that life only needed to start once to be a success. There was no requirement for several life forms to appear independently to create the wealth of biodiversity we now enjoy. Natural selection was powerful enough to make everything from one source only. In addition, once a life form had appeared, its success would make it impossible for the process to repeat. Whatever resources that made the appearance of life possible would now be used more efficiently by that primitive life form. There was simply no opportunity left for an alternative form of life to join in after that.

Did life come from space?

The question is still open though: Where did the ancient common ancestor come from?

The logical answer is that organic life has an inorganic origin. However, even before Darwin's work, people were suggesting that the common ancestor need not be an Earthling. Earth could have been seeded by primitive life forms coming from space—or at the very least the complex chemicals that it uses, such as DNA. This rather wild theory suggests Earth's life arrived inside the ice core of a comet or locked within meteorite rocks streaking through the atmosphere. The idea is known as "panspermia," meaning "seeds from everywhere." It might sound a little ridiculous, I mean, what are the odds?

Life on a simmer

When it comes to the origin of life, we are dealing with very long odds indeed. If chemicals were to arrange themselves into a body-sized cluster, there are billions of ways they could do it that were not alive and only a very few that would qualify as living. However, when we take into account scale and size of the universe, those long odds take on a different meaning. It is bound to happen at some point. So when it comes to the origins of life, the chance of Earth's life coming from space is not beyond the realm of possibility.

Putting aside panspermia for now (we'll get back to it later), we should return to tracing a likely route that allowed chemical processes to create the first biological processes. It is proposed that this began on Earth around 3.8 billion years ago. At this point, Earth had cooled enough to have a permanent ocean. The search for the origins of life start by hypothesizing the likely conditions of the young Earth. We then add time (we have a lot of that) and see what happens. This process has led to two possible theories: life was cooked in a soup or baked in a rock.

The cooking theory came first, and the concept arose from an experiment performed in 1953 by an ex-nuclear physicist named Harold Urey and a chemist called Stanley Miller. They had the idea of building a tiny version of Earth's lifeless ocean, stocked with the simple inorganic chemicals they believed would be present. They took their ingredient list from the chemicals that were by then being seen across the universe, things like carbon dioxide, methane, and ammonia. These were all mixed into a substance that is very common on Earth but is actually very rare in the universe—liquid water. This combination has become known as the primordial soup, and Miller and Urey planned to re-create the conditions of early Earth and see what happened to it.

Their experiment was carried out in an apparatus dubbed the "lollipop." It earned this name from its main reaction chamber, which was a rounded glass flask with a series of pipes entering and leaving it. The apparatus pumped the primordial soup into and out of the lollipop, and as it traveled around the closed loop, the mixture was boiled, stirred, cooled, and electrified to simulate lightning. This was an attempt to re-create the kinds of changeable conditions that existed in Earth's oceans before life existed.

The lollipop

The lollipop was left running constantly for several days. From the outside, the clear liquid was seen to become a cloudy pink and a residue appeared. After a week, Miller and Urey examined the products of their experiment. They found that many of the raw materials had been converted into the familiar chemical building blocks of life, such as amino acids and simple carbohydrates.

This posed the question: If the lollipop was run for millions of years on a much larger scale would complex materials, such as nucleic acid chains and proteins, be produced?

The benchmark for life is an autocatalysing chemical. Think back to our proofs of life from chapter 1. An RNA molecule is able to build a copy of itself from the constituent raw materials in the water around it. This process is called autocatalysis. A catalyst is a chemical that facilitates reactions that would not happen (or happen very slowly) without it. However, the catalyst is not used up the process. So RNA is a catalyst for the reactions that are required to build an identical version of itself.

> 66 An RNA molecule is able to build a copy of itself from the constituent raw materials in the water around it. 99

RNA is tough stuff compared to DNA, and it is conjectured that DNA did not evolve until after the arrival of cellular life (more on that later), so it is likely that we are all descended from a piece of RNA. However, it is unlikely that RNA was the first autocatalysing chemical in the primordial soup (if the soup theory is correct, that is).

Instead, a whole host of nucleic acids were likely to have existed and competed with each other for resources. This is natural selection at its most raw, and the result was a period of chemical evolution where species of nucleic acids arose by mutation, driving others to extinction. RNA, or something like it, was able to team up with simple proteins that may have been evolving in a similar parallel process. The proteins worked to strengthen and protect the nucleic acid and helped with replication. The competing nucleic acids were becoming more like today's viruses in form (but not function).

Structure of DNA & RNA

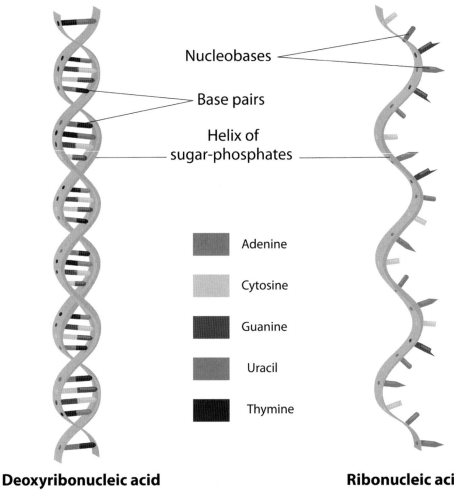

Nucleobases

Base pairs

Helix of
sugar-phosphates

Adenine

Cytosine

Guanine

Uracil

Thymine

**Deoxyribonucleic acid
(DNA)**

**Ribonucleic acid
(RNA)**

Remember RNA (ribonucleic acid) is a polymer of nucleic acids. Let's say that another way: RNA is a long chain of molecules made up of small units known as nucleic acids, which are all strung together along a backbone of ribose sugar molecules. RNA uses four nucleic acids, and the sequence of these nucleic acids can vary from one RNA molecule to another. During its chemical evolution, the sequence of its acid units became linked to the fine structure of its protein helpers. A change, or mutation, in the RNA sequence resulted in a change in the structure and shape of a protein that coated the RNA. Most of the time that was a disaster, but occasionally the change was a boost to the chemical cluster. The coded sequences held within the long RNA molecule became genes. Chemical evolution had given way to genetic evolution.

> RNA is a long chain of molecules made up of small units known as nucleic acids, which are all strung together along a backbone of ribose sugar molecules.

The next step was to shroud the nucleic acid in a lipid membrane, where it could hoard its supply of resources. In other words, it built a cell. Lipids (or fats) have a rather interesting characteristic: one half of the molecule is immiscible in water; the other half dissolves. A cell membrane is a double layer of lipid molecules. The water-repelling parts of each lipid layer mingle with each other, while the water-loving parts create the external faces of the membrane. Such a membrane is relatively fragile and can be strengthened

by the inclusion of proteins, but the first cells were likely
thousands of times smaller than the cells in your body.

RNA cannot form a double helix, unlike DNA. DNA may have
existed before the evolution of cells, or it may have evolved
after as a way of improving the accuracy of the replication
process. A double helix is a good way of protecting the genetic
code because it is shielded inside the twin strands of the
molecule. A huge length of DNA—often looped into what is
called a plasmid—was able to store many more genes safely
compared to their RNA cousins. However, when it came to
reading and transmitting the information the genes contained
and making the proteins, RNA was better suited to those
processes. Today your cells do the same: DNA in the nucleus of
each cell is the information store, while RNA is various guises
works to turn that information into a living organism.

> " DNA may have existed
> before the evolution
> of cells, or it may have
> evolved after as a way of
> improving the accuracy of
> the replication process. "

Cells like yours evolved at least a billion years after the
very first cells, which were more like those of bacteria.
In fact, it is thought that your cells are actually teams of
bacterial cells that evolved to work together inside one
single membrane. To do that the cell membrane needed to
incorporate cholesterol molecules, which made it flexible

but strong and allowed the cells to be hundreds, if not thousands, of times more voluminous than their bacterial forebears. (Cholesterol may be one of life's enduring problems for many people, but without it, we would not have made it beyond bacteria.)

This team-building event, known as "endosymbiosis," may have happened several times. It was undoubtedly rare. However, every organism with a cell of this kind evolved from a single ancestor. The other teams have not made it. The organisms with cells like this are called the "eukaryotes," and they include everything from a humble single-celled amoeba to a mighty oak tree, a blue whale, and you.

> The organisms with cells like this are called the eukaryotes, and they include everything from a humble single-celled amoeba to a mighty oak tree, blue whale, and you.

The smaller, more primitive cells are called "prokaryotes." These include bacteria, which despite their tiny size pack a punch. The weight of the world's bacteria equals the weight of all plants and animals combined!

However, bacteria are not the only prokaryotes. In 1978, a new kind of life was discovered. They are the class Archaea. To you and me they look like bacteria, but analysis of their biochemistry shows that they had split from bacteria way back near to the dawn of cellular life. The first archaea were found in the waters gushing from hydrothermal vents on the deep seabed. This water is extremely warm—easily hot enough to scald us—but the archaea were perfectly happy living in it. These strange bugs are called "extremophiles"— lovers of extremes—and they are found in places of extreme temperatures, high salt contents, and other habitats that are too much for the rest of life to survive. This got people thinking about the nature of the young Earth around the time when life evolved. Could it be that these extremophiles are the living descendants of the first cells?

Your ancestors

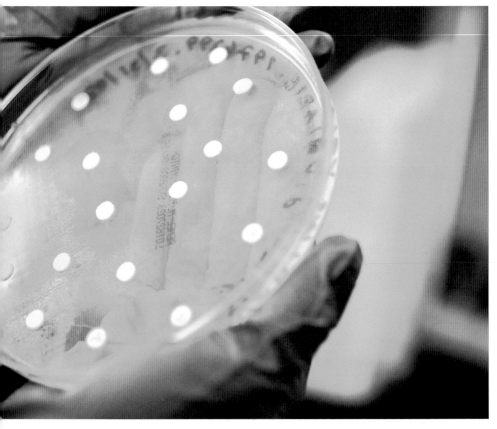

THE
BIG ANSWER

Hydrothermal vents were first discovered on the seabed in the 1960s. They are hot springs in the seabed, where water that has percolated deep into the rocks is heated at great pressure by volcanic activity deep underground. This hot water, laden with chemicals, spurts out of cracks in the seabed creating "smokers" (either black or white) as they meet the cold ocean and release their chemical loads.

A hydrothermal vent

In 1977, human explorers visited a black smoker near the Galapagos Islands, and perhaps fittingly for that location, they discovered an entirely new kind of ecosystem down there previously thought impossible. The smoker was in the midnight zone, so called because sunlight never gets down that far. It is always dark, and no photosynthetic life can live there. Deep sea animals can survive on "marine snow," which is the euphemism for the shower of dead bodies that sinks from the sun-lit surface water to the bottom. This source of food is nevertheless the fruits of an ecosystem powered by the sun.

> " Deep sea animals can survive on "marine snow," which is the euphemism for the shower of dead bodies that sinks from the sun-lit surface water to the bottom. "

Until the vent was visited, it was thought that all life on Earth received its energy, however far removed, from a primary producer trapping a twinkle of sunlight in its cells. However, the animals that lived around the vent were getting their energy from another source— chemosynthetic bacteria (or more correctly archaea), which used chemicals in the volcanic water.

This discovery has been combined with another to propose a second theory about where life really started.

> 66 We live in an oxygenated world now because autotrophs changed the biosphere, but organisms that evolved before this "Great Oxygenation Event," did not use oxygen like us. 99

Around 2.3 billion years ago, Earth's rocks began to change. Oxide minerals, such as hematite (iron ore), ruby, and periclase began to appear. To form, these need free oxygen. Oxygen is very reactive stuff, and it does not hang around for long before it reacts. However, the geological evidence shows that the supply of oxygen just kept on coming until it stabilized at about 20 percent of the atmosphere. The source of this oxygen? Life itself.

Many autotrophs had cracked photosynthesis by this time and were changing the chemistry of Earth's biosphere in the process. We live in an oxygenated world now because autrotrophs changed the biosphere, but organisms that evolved before this "Great Oxygenation Event," did not use oxygen like us. In fact, it killed them in what must have been the most devastating die off the world has seen.

Life before photosynthesis must have used something other than the raw materials of carbon dioxide, oxygen, water, glucose, and assorted minerals that underlies life today (there are a few more requirements, but you get the picture). Could it be that these early life forms were much more like the extremophiles of the deep-sea vents, living off chemicals such as ammonia, methane, and sulphides?

This brought the primordial soup back into question. While we regard the oceans as the birth place of life, was it really at the surface or in the shallow sunlit seas where it all happened? That is certainly the location of the so-called Cambrian Explosion that saw the evolution of most of today's plant and animal communities, but that was just more than 500 million years ago. Life has been around a lot longer than that, and more than 4 billion years ago, the oceans were a lot less stable than they are now. It is likely that they boiled away several times due to meteor bombardments in the early days, and once the waters became a permanent fixture did they really thicken up into a reactive goop chock full of prebiotic chemicals? Perhaps in some locations, and the prime candidate for this is now seen as the seabed.

> " Life has been around a lot longer than 500 million years, and 4 billion years ago, the oceans were a lot less stable than they are now. "

Research over the last few decades has focused on the role of sediments, particularly clay ones. These materials can hold water and other chemicals in tiny pores between grains of sediment and offer a huge surface area where reacting chemicals can meet. Also, the deep sediments were largely protected from the turmoil taking place at the surface of Earth. Many biochemists now believe that clay sediments acted as some kind of bioreactor for chemical evolution, where conditions were right for RNA to evolve and where the first life used chemosynthesis to power its metabolism in ways used by extremophiles today.

Perhaps the best way to confirm how life started on Earth is to look for it on other worlds. The extremophile-based theories suggest that life does not necessarily need a total doppelgänger of Earth to get going, and so perhaps we will find evidence of life in all kinds of places—some not so far away.

Is clay the cradle of life?

Q5

IS **EARTH** THE ONLY PLACE **WITH LIFE**?

The hubbub of our telecommunicating civilization is leaking out into space. Is anyone getting the messages? It is often said that Adolf Hitler's TV broadcast of the opening ceremony of the 1936 Berlin Olympics used radio signals powerful enough to travel beyond the atmosphere and enter space. Are these grainy black and white images leading the way, carrying evidence of humanity's existence into deep space?

66 For a message to reach the next star system and beyond, it will need to be sent on purpose, formed into a powerful directed beam. 99

Technically yes, the Nazi broadcasts were powerful enough to get into space, but they were not designed to carry a signal any great distance. The faintest trace of the signals will have long since dissipated into the background. For a message to reach the next star system and beyond, it will need to be sent on purpose, formed into a powerful directed beam. So what kind of things do our messages to the stars say?

In 1974, information about DNA, the solar system, and our mathematics system was combined into a pictorial message. The graphic was high tech by 1970s standards but looks much like a screen from a rudimentary video game. A certain simplicity was required so the receiver of the message could figure it all out. The signal was broadcast from the Arecibo radio telescope in Puerto Rico, an impressive dish built inside a sinkhole in the jungle. It was directed at a cluster of stars in the Hercules constellation. That is 2,200 light years away, meaning it will be available for detection in the year 4174. Assuming our new Herculean chums get back to us straight away, we should hear from them in the year 6374.

Sending messages to aliens

More recently a Doritos commercial was sent to a newly discovered planetary system in Ursa Major (the Plough or Big Dipper).

Even if any viewer of the commercial likes corn-based snacks, they will have trouble getting a delivery. Today's fastest spacecraft travel twenty thousand times slower than radio signals. A journey to the nearest star beyond the sun would take eighty thousand years.

> 66 Astronomers have already cued up an entirely new scientific field to study life on other worlds. It is called "**exobiology**." 99

So here is the issue at hand: If intelligent life existed far out in the universe, could we ever make contact? Could they ever return our call, and would it be possible to ever meet? Some space scientists counsel against sending more advanced calling cards into space in the first place. If they were picked up by an alien race capable of acting on them, they are likely to have a much more advanced technology than us. We have been playing around with radio waves since the 1890s. We have gone a long way since then, but perhaps there is already an interstellar broadcast network and our antennae are not able to pick it up. A civilization able to send a broadcast like that would also have the ability to wipe us out with relative ease. They may not want to of course, but why take the chance?

Other commentators say that the odds are against ever finding a friend (or enemy) in space are very slim. Civilizations come and go—our sun won't last forever, folks. Even if intelligent life was common in the universe (there are reasons to expect it may not be), the chances of a civilization being in the right place at the right time to respond to our calls is very slim indeed.

However, aliens don't have to be space-traveling little green men. Green slime would be enough—as long as it is alive.

Carbon complexity

Astronomers have already cued up an entirely new scientific field to study life on other worlds. It is called "exobiology." However, there are no exobiologists yet, because we have not found any alien life. The search is the job of another group, called "astrobiologists."

> 66 Life makes use of about 5,000 compounds, and only 250 of those are not carbon based. 99

Where do you start looking for aliens when you have the whole universe to choose from? The first assumptions are that life must be carbon based and require a supply of liquid water.

Earth's life is carbon based and there is sound chemistry that suggests all life has to use this as its primary element. Carbon is the first member of Group 4 in the periodic table (some versions have it at 14). As a member of Group 4, one carbon atom can form four chemical bonds with other atoms. However, it is not restricted to four bonds. It can also form double, even triple bonds, with certain atoms (mostly other carbons). This flexibility allows carbon molecules to form as chains, rings, and more complex three-dimensional branched networks.

It is not just the constituent atoms that give a molecule its characteristics but also its shape, and with carbon it is possible to arrange the same ingredients in many different ways. As a result, of the 10 million compounds catalogued by chemists, 9 million of them are carbon based. Life makes use of about 5,000 compounds, and only 250 of those are not carbon based.

> " Earth is in a Goldilocks orbit. That means it is not too hot, not too cold, but just right for liquid water to exist on the surface. "

The other members of Group 4 include silicon, germanium, tin, and lead. All of them can form four bonds in a molecule, so why can't life be based on lead or silicon? The answer is that carbon's atoms are considerably smaller than the others, and so they are able to form tight bonds that are strong enough to stay together inside the immense chemical structures found in living bodies. To some extent silicon (the next smallest in the group) can form chains and branched molecules. These are known as silanes and are analogous to propane and butane, the stuff in lighters and camping stoves. However, silicon's bonds are not strong enough to hold together molecules with dozens, let alone millions, of atoms.

So, carbon is the only option. Luckily there is a lot of it about. Even the most average of stars makes some as it enters its final billion years or so.

Water is also highly abundant—its hydrogen was formed in the big bang, its oxygen was made in stars along with the carbon. However, liquid water is a much more elusive substance. There has been no direct observation of liquid water beyond our planet, although distant solar systems have been identified where it may exist.

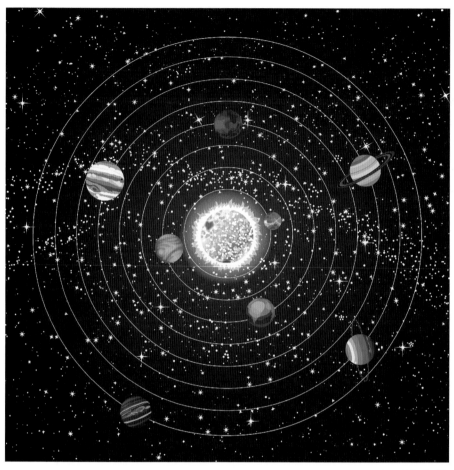

Just right for life

Astrobiology takes its cue from Earth and draws in knowledge from geology, chemistry, and biology to figure out where might be a good place to look for life beyond our world. The limits of space travel mean that astrobiologists have no plans to send missions beyond the solar system, but never fear; they have pinpointed a few places in our own local space neighborhood where conditions might be able to harbor life.

Earth is in a Goldilocks orbit. That means it is not too hot, not too cold, but just right for liquid water to exist on the surface. There is only room for one planet here, so all the other bodies in the solar system do not have water on the surface. Farther in toward the sun, Venus is too warm and all the water exists as vapor. (It does rain on Venus, but it is concentrated sulphuric acid—and it seldom falls all the way to the surface.) Mercury is blasted by hot solar wind and is too small to hold on to any atmosphere. Its surface is bone dry, although its strange orbital behavior—its day is longer than its year—means that some of its deeper craters are in perpetual shadow. Down there, it may be cold enough for water ice to survive even that close to the sun.

> Two or three billion years ago, the processes that were creating life on Earth may have been running in parallel on Mars.

Ice is more common on bodies orbiting farther out from Earth. Mars was considered as the place where aliens were most likely to come from. In whimsical premodern times, the general idea was that Venus was home to beautiful beings who lived in a tropical paradise, while Mars was populated by a hardened spartan race. In order to survive on the red planet, they had become industrious, organized, and belligerent.

Depictions of Martians have been part of popular culture for centuries.

In 1877, the Italian astronomer Giovanni Schiaparelli capitalized on Mars passing close to Earth to take a good look. He drew a map of the surface as he saw it, and when published in English, his labels for "canali," or channels, were translated as "canals"—artificial waterways. This error caught the imagination of astronomers and the public at large. H.G. Wells was inspired to write *The War of the Worlds* twenty years later. By doing so, he sealed the fate of the Martians; they were to be the bad guys in the solar system for the next three generations. Meanwhile, Percival Lowell, a wealthy American businessman, built an entire observatory at Flagstaff, Arizona, to scour Mars for more evidence of Martians. (He found nothing there, but after his death, his observatory did detect Pluto, then regarded as the ninth planet.)

When the Viking landers arrived on the surface of Mars just under a century after Schiaparelli's observations, they found a cold, lifeless desert.

However, it is thought that Mars had had an atmosphere similar to the young Earth's in the past, and there is evidence that liquid water once flowed over its surface. Two or three billion years ago, the processes that were creating life on Earth may have been running in parallel on Mars. Mars is most likely a dead planet now, but the rovers that scour its surface may yet find evidence of long-gone Martian life fossilized in the rocks.

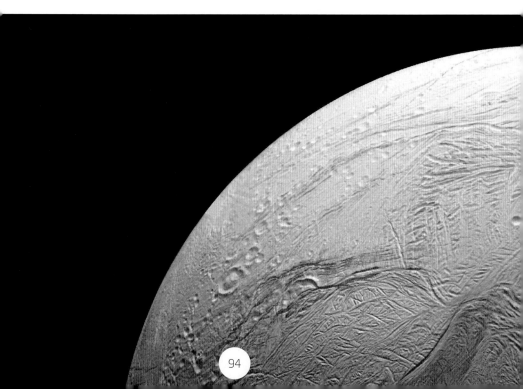

Farther out still, there is hope that abiogenic processes such as the ones that are thought to have occurred in the chemical-rich sediments of Earth may still be present. The prime candidates are Europa, a moon of Jupiter; and Enceladus, which orbits Saturn.

> " Europa is more substantial and just slightly smaller than the Moon in size. "

Enceladus is very, very small. It would quite happily fit on top of Spain. Europa is more substantial and just slightly smaller than the Moon. Both Europa and Enceladus are ice moons. Instead of rocks their surfaces are covered in a crust of ice. On both, our fly-by probes have observed powerful geysers sending out vast jets of water. This tells us that the moons have some source of internal heat that is driving this volcanic, hydrothermal activity. And that means that beneath the ice crust is a hidden ocean of liquid water, and under that is a core of chemical-rich rocks.

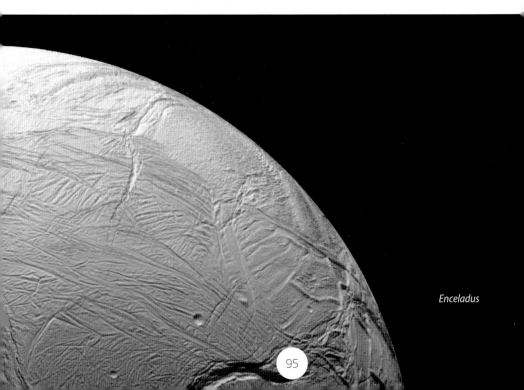

Enceladus

The ocean on Enceladus is a relatively small pocket about 6 miles (10 km) deep that lies around the southern pole. Europa's ocean surrounds the entire core, and amazingly its volume is calculated to exceed that of Earth's ocean. Astrobiologists wonder whether hydrothermal vents are on the seabeds of either moon, and if so, whether life has emerged around them.

To find out will be a difficult undertaking. A lander that is half spaceship and half drilling rig will need to be sent to each moon. To avoid having to drill through many thousands of feet of ice—something we find difficult on Earth—astrobiologists propose targeting fractured regions where liquid water may rise close to the surface.

> " Is Earth, the living planet, rather mediocre and banal, or is it very special and rare, perhaps even unique? "

If it were possible to reach an alien ocean, our probe would run the risk of contaminating the water with hardy lifeforms transported from Earth. How the water would be collected safely is an open problem. And then it would need to be analyzed—perhaps even brought back to Earth.

There are no concrete plans to send such a probe, although NASA is working on it. With luck, a probe will be on its way to Europa by the mid-2020s. Perhaps it will tell us we are not alone in the universe. However, until then the debate continues: Is Earth, the living planet, rather mediocre and banal, or is it very special and rare, perhaps even unique?

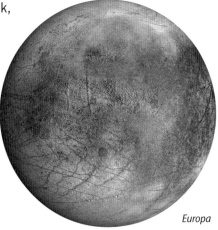

Europa

THE
BIG ANSWER

In 1990, the *Voyager 1* probe was 3.7 billion miles (6 billion km) from Earth. Its main mission to survey the outer planets was complete. It then left to head out of the solar system and become the first artificial object to ever reach interstellar space. It is still going, carrying a golden gramophone record filled with coded audio and images of Earth. That was the brainchild of astronomer and writer Carl Sagan, meant as a time-capsule from Earth should *Voyager* be found by an alien civilization millions of years in the future.

> " In 1990, the *Voyager 1* probe was was 3.7 billion miles (6 billion km) from Earth. Its main mission to survey the outer planets was complete. "

As *Voyager* sped away from its final rendezvous with Neptune in 1990, Sagan had another idea. He asked that *Voyager* be swung around to face back toward Earth and take a picture from the edge of known space. The resulting image is called the Pale Blue Dot. There is not much to see, and that was Sagan's intention.

Sagan's picture summed up the Copernican principle, which is named after Nicholas Copernicus. In the sixteenth century, this Polish priest calculated that Earth and the planets must orbit the sun and not, as had been assumed until then, that the sun, the moon, and everything else in the universe moved around Earth. Copernicus's breakthrough shifted our planet from the center of the universe, and that not only revolutionized astronomy and all other sciences, it also changed the way humans saw themselves.

Copernicus, the man who put Earth in its place

The Copernican principle, also known as the principle of mediocrity, extends that shift to what we have learned about the universe since. The solar system is by no means near the middle of the universe, it is on the outer fringe of a galaxy called the Milky Way. The Milky Way contains many billions of stars and is one of hundreds of billion of galaxies estimated to exist in the universe. Compared to all that, Earth is just a Pale Blue Dot.

> " The solar system is by no means near the middle of the universe; it is on the outer fringe of a galaxy called the Milky Way. "

However, people clung to the idea that the solar system was still rather special. Where else had such a wonderful family of planets? In 2009, the Kepler space telescope was launched to have a look for some. These were not planets that orbited our sun, but satellites of distant stars—exoplanets. The Kepler mission was astoundingly successful. In four years, the telescope found good evidence of 450 solar systems with exoplanets. Some of these exoplanets were the size of Earth and were in the equivalent of their particular star's Goldilocks orbit, better described as the habitable zone. Extrapolating the data, it is likely that stars without any planets are the exception, and that the Milky Way contains more planets than stars! A staggering 40 billion of these exoplanets could be Earthlike—the right size and in the right place for life to exist. There may be a lot of blue dots out there!

Earth is undoubtedly important—to us at least. Where else are we going to go? However, there is another school of thought that attempts to put us back up in the A-list of heavenly bodies. In 2000, Peter Ward, a geologist and paleontologist, and Donald E. Brownlee, and astronomer, put forward the rare Earth theory. The gist of it was something like this: life on Earth has been through three phases. First was the origin of life in the form of simple prokaryotic single-celled organisms. Then endosymbiosis allowed for larger cells that could work together in multicellular bodies. Finally, a species became intelligent enough to understand what had

An Earthlike exoplanet

just happened. The suggestion is not that this is the inevitable climax of natural selection. Evolution has no direction. However, the three phases nevertheless require a huge span of time, and there is little scope for interruption. They suggest that despite the possibility of life arising on exoplanets being quite high, only a planet with the very special characteristics of Earth could produce a civilization.

> The solar system is far from the galactic center, and is therefore less affected by the violent activities that go on in that more crowded region.

Here is some of their reasoning. The sun is a yellow dwarf—nothing special about it at all. However, a star of this size burns slowly and lasts about 10 billion years (we are halfway through). A larger star burns hotter and brighter but can burn out in a fraction of the time—not enough for life to develop from primordial germs to civilized gentlefolk. So we can wipe a few billion off our list of Earthlike planets. Their stars are too big.

The solar system is far from the galactic center, and is therefore less affected by the violent activities that go on in that more crowded region. Gamma ray bursts and radiation from black holes would be a major hazard for life developing in this area. It is probable that life itself would survive the periodic blasts from space. (Some suspect that the Great Dying, the largest mass extinction event seen on Earth about 250 million years ago, which saw 96 percent of marine life wiped out and 70 percent of land organisms killed, was caused by the gamma rays produced by a huge supernova.) However if life was repeatedly knocked back, its rate of development—in whatever directions it was heading— would be slower.

The rare Earth hypothesis points to many other factors, such as the position of Jupiter. This gas giant is in just the right place to protect Earth from the worst meteorite impacts. Anything big is swept up by Jupiter before it gets near us—although some get through, just ask a dinosaur. However, Jupiter is not too close, otherwise it would destabilize Earth's orbit.

> " Anything big is swept up by Jupiter before it gets near us—although some get through, just ask a dinosaur. "

So accordingly, we could remove planets in the middle of the galaxy and ones that are not supported by a big brother planet—but one that is not too overbearing. At a guess the number of "civilized" planets is now quite low.

Earth also has a very large moon for a planet of its size. The best theory of how it got one is that soon after its formation, the young Earth was given a glancing blow by another planet about the size of Mars. This hypothetical planet is called Theia, the mother goddess of the moon in Greek mythology. If Theia had hit more directly, Earth would have been obliterated. As luck would have it, the impact was just right to knock off a chunk of Earth's mantle which accreted into the moon. (The impact would have also blown away some of the atmosphere, allowing Earth to shed heat faster, making it more suited to its habitable zone orbit.) The chances of another exoplanet forming a similar giant moon in the same way must be incredibly small—our list is shrinking again. Our moon boosts the tides, doubling the gravitational pull that makes the oceans rise and fall each day. Tidal zones are hotbeds of evolution, providing refuge for marine animals to escape from predators in the water, and then becoming the halfway house between an aquatic life and a terrestrial one. Without the moon, terrestrial life may have taken much longer to evolve, although that does not preclude the possibility of civilization appearing in a marine environment.

> " The chances of another exoplanet forming a similar giant moon in the same way must be incredibly small— our list is shrinking again. "

Ward and Brownlee went so far as to build an equation for estimating the chance of a planet being a "rare Earth" like ours. We won't go into it here, but it goes without saying the figure is very low.

The rare Earth hypothesis has many detractors but it ably highlights one undeniable fact. If we do find alien life, we are likely to be the only beings who will know it.

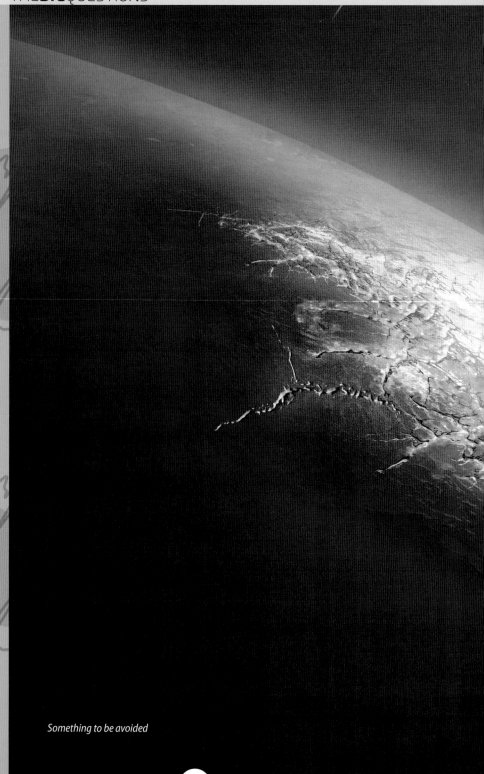

Something to be avoided

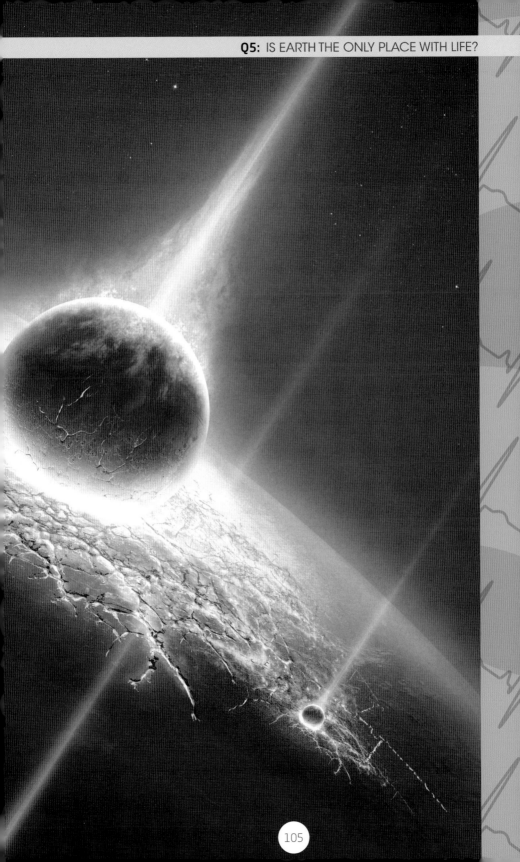

Q6

WHAT IS A
NEAR-DEATH
EXPERIENCE?

> "Death is nothing to us, since when we are, death has not come, and when death has come, we are not."

"Death is nothing to us, since when we are, death has not come, and when death has come, we are not." So said Epicurus in the third century BCE. The affable Greek philosopher was expounding his theories about living a good life. To him, the goal of life was to pursue pleasure, not by feeding hedonistic desires, mind you, but through a thoughtful, pleasant existence filled with good deeds, decent conversation, and kindness. To achieve happiness, he reasoned, first one had to give up the fear of death. All that we know of death, Epicurus was saying, is that it is not life, and therefore death should not be something to be concerned about. We are incapable of experiencing what it is like to be dead. If we could experience it, then we are not really dead.

However, not everyone agreed with him then, and nor do they agree now. To them, death is not the end. By that reasoning, the term "life" refers to a limited corporeal existence in a physical universe. Upon death, that phase of existence ends, but something of the person continues, or survives death. What that existence might be like is for another time (chapter 11 to be exact), but what on earth (or in heaven) is it that leads one to question the bald Epicurean logic?

Although they are fascinating subjects in their own right, we will have to ignore the contributions of the hunch, prophecy, faith, or intuition. These offer no explanation that can be tested. All of them are informed, however, by a phenomenon that lies right of the crossroads between mysticism, faith, science, and medicine: the near-death experience (NDE).

Firstly, we need to deal with a bit of sophistry. Someone who has undergone a near-death experience is often said to have died and come back to life. We cannot have this. Putting aside a few supernatural

> "The experience often takes them to another realm, where their sensations are more acute than in life and where they meet kindly beings or perhaps dead members of their family."

beings and spiritual heads of world religions, death has to be a permanent state. On death, a body has become incapable of life. The marvelous skill of doctors and their medical technologies means that the point of death has been moved. A malfunctioning body can perhaps be restarted after its signs of life have faded away, and perhaps that can be achieved many minutes or even hours after normal functioning has ceased. However, the body is dead only once all attempts to save it have ended.

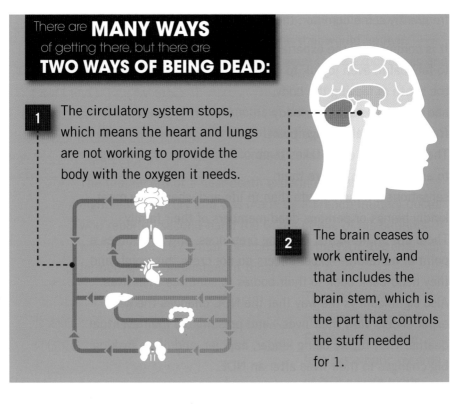

There are **MANY WAYS** of getting there, but there are **TWO WAYS OF BEING DEAD:**

1 The circulatory system stops, which means the heart and lungs are not working to provide the body with the oxygen it needs.

2 The brain ceases to work entirely, and that includes the brain stem, which is the part that controls the stuff needed for 1.

The first scenario can be averted using life support machines, which take over that function. The brain cannot be replaced by an external support system. If brain death is suspected, doctors do a brain scan involving radioactive markers. Death is clear to see when none of those markers appear inside the brain.

responders from the 1960s onwards. As a result, the point of death was pushed back further, than at any point in history. People could stop breathing, their heart could stop for several minutes, and with the right care they could be saved. The point of death began to recede further and the number of reports of NDEs, although still low, began to rise.

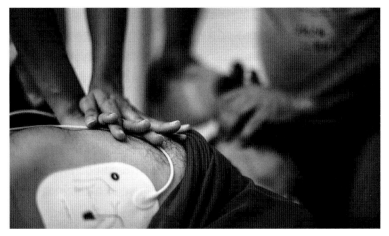

CPR being administered to a patient near to death

This leads us to think that the near-death experience is a new phenomenon, not one that went by another name in pre-modern times. It has only been in the last few decades that medical science has been so able to pull people back from the brink of death.

Doctors are focused on preventing death, and few have an interest in studying death itself, but by the 1980s, the field of "near-death studies" was established (in a small way). A wide range of researchers from psychiatrists and brain scientists to those with "alternative" techniques have been probing the NDE to see what it might tell us. For some, the NDE is evidence of some unseen characteristic of the universe that is being revealed at death. Others do not research the NDE to find out about death, but life.

In 1983, Bruce Greyson, a U.S. psychiatrist, developed a scale to quantify a near-death experience.

Research subjects were asked the following questions:

1. Did time seem to speed up or slow down?

2. Were your thoughts speeded up?

3. Did scenes from your past come back to you?

4. Did you suddenly seem to understand everything?

5. Did you have a feeling of peace or pleasantness?

6. Did you have a feeling of joy?

7. Did you feel a sense of harmony or unity with the universe?

8. Did you see, or feel surrounded by, a brilliant light?

9. Were your senses more vivid than usual?

10. Did you seem to be aware of things going on elsewhere, as if by extrasensory perception (ESP)?

11. Did scenes from the future come to you?

12. Did you feel separated from your body?

13. Did you seem to enter some other, unearthly world?

14. Did you seem to encounter a mystical being or presence, or hear an unidentifiable voice?

15. Did you see deceased or religious spirits?

16. Did you come to a border or point of no return?

Their answers earn them a score of 0 to 2 for each question. Any score above 7 is regarded as an NDE.

collecting a host of sensory inputs and associating them into a mental model of the body's posture. Yet, there is a disconnect between this sensory model and the motor system used to control posture. One of the key inputs on posture comes from the muscles themselves. But this component is missing from the associative model in the brain. As a result, the person's brain has two competing perceptions of where the body is—one from the relaxed muscles, the other from the other sensory information. Consequently, one of those models is perceived to be outside of the body and is felt as another presence nearby.

> " However, the waking brain has become aware of its body. This involves collecting a host of sensory inputs and associating them into a mental model of the body's posture. "

So there are a lot of conflicting theories and information about what the near-death experience can mean. Is it evidence of the soul leaving the body and heading for the next phase of its existence, or is it an artifact of the dying brain? Or could it be both?

In 1983, Bruce Greyson, a U.S. psychiatrist, developed a scale to quantify a near-death experience.

Research subjects were asked the following questions:

1. Did time seem to speed up or slow down?

2. Were your thoughts speeded up?

3. Did scenes from your past come back to you?

4. Did you suddenly seem to understand everything?

5. Did you have a feeling of peace or pleasantness?

6. Did you have a feeling of joy?

7. Did you feel a sense of harmony or unity with the universe?

8. Did you see, or feel surrounded by, a brilliant light?

9. Were your senses more vivid than usual?

10. Did you seem to be aware of things going on elsewhere, as if by extrasensory perception (ESP)?

11. Did scenes from the future come to you?

12. Did you feel separated from your body?

13. Did you seem to enter some other, unearthly world?

14. Did you seem to encounter a mystical being or presence, or hear an unidentifiable voice?

15. Did you see deceased or religious spirits?

16. Did you come to a border or point of no return?

Their answers earn them a score of 0 to 2 for each question. Any score above 7 is regarded as an NDE.

NDEs make great tales, especially when combined with the redemption stories of transformed lives that follow them. For the well-publicized NDEs, the experience has done what Epicurus had advised all along: it has taught us that one has nothing to fear from death. However, we hear almost nothing of the NDEs that tell a different story, one of despair, terror, and pain. It is thought that a quarter of all NDEs are like this, but people are less willing talk about them.

This is the major issue with the study of NDEs. Almost all of the data comes from a self-selecting group of people, who come forward to talk about their experience. Many will have had their NDE years before, and they have recalled and retold it many times since. This raises the possibility that the memories become faulty. The phrase "faulty memory" sounds rather Orwellian, but what we mean is that with every retelling, the recounted version of the event becomes the one remembered, and this will always differ slightly from the original experience. Over the years, the gist of it all can diverge somewhat.

Leaving the body

What is it that turns an NDE from a life-changing fantasy into an account of a verifiable historical event? We are not using the term "fantasy" in a pejorative sense but purely to indicate that NDEs may all take place inside someone's imagination. The word that researchers want to use is "**veridical**."

> " After her recovery, Maria told nurses of her NDE and in particular about a sneaker on a window ledge outside the window. "

A veridical experience is one that is capable of verification against real events. Do NDEs contain any veridical elements? A return to the NDE scale above will tell you that most of an NDE is based outside of objective reality as experiencers visit dead relatives and divine realms. However, the out-of-body experience, where a person reports watching themselves in hospital (or somewhere) being attended to by the medics who will save their lives is a well-worn trope of the NDE. However, this component is actually quite rare among reports of NDEs. Nevertheless, what veridical components have been reported?

None.

There are a few tantalizing possibilities. A lead contender comes from 1977, when a patient called Maria was critically ill in a Seattle hospital. After her recovery, Maria told nurses of her NDE and in particular about a sneaker on a window ledge outside the window. It was later confirmed that the shoe was indeed there and in such a position that it could not be seen from inside the room. So why does this not count as a veridical experience? Maria was never interviewed by NDE researchers, and her account was told second-hand by her social worker.

That is not enough for it to pass any objective test.

Another famous case often referred to in NDE circles relates to an American singer called Pam Reynolds. In 1991, Reynolds had a brain surgery and her entire body was chilled to 60°F (15°C), well below its normal working temperature. This had the effect of stopping her heart, so the surgeons could drain the blood from her head. However, the cold temperature was meant to preserve her body so it could be re-infused and the heart restarted after the operation.

> " This is the rather terrifying idea that about 1 in every 1,000 patients becomes aware of their surroundings during an operation. "

Reynolds was connected to an EEG to record her brain activity. The anesthesiologist was particularly interested in watching for activity in the hind brain, where the basic functions of life are managed. Throughout the operation, loud clicks were played into Reynolds's seemingly lifeless ears. These were a meant as a powerful stimulus that would show up on the EEG if the patient's brain began to function during the operation. It did not.

After the operation, Reynolds was able to recall many details from the operating room, such as pieces of conversation between the surgical team and the songs they were listening to. Advocates of NDEs have used her first-hand account as the best example yet of a veridical experience. However, closer scrutiny of the timeline of her operation shows that many of her memories of the procedure are related to events that happened at the beginning and end of the operation—or could be constructed from those events. It is probable that Reynolds had experienced anesthesia awareness. This is the rather terrifying idea that about 1 in every 1,000 patients becomes aware of their surroundings during an operation. It's a sliding scale, so we are not talking about people sitting bolt upright on the operating table, but anesthetics do not usher everyone behind the curtain of unconsciousness in the same way. Some still see and hear things through the gaps. That is why an anesthesiologist is always on hand to keep you under.

To some, the Pam Reynolds case shows that the mind survives the apparent death of the body. Others say it was all in her imagination, elaborated on by her semiconscious observations before and after her surgery.

> " Any interviews must happen as soon as possible to prevent the possibility of memories being tarnished and confused after the event. "

In the last decade, there have been attempts to put the study of NDEs on a more thorough scientific footing. Rather than waiting for experiencers to come and tell their stories—or answer a call to—researchers have been asking survivors of cardiac arrests to report any experiences right after the event. This is fraught with difficulty. Any interviews must happen as soon as possible to prevent the possibility of memories being tarnished and confused after the event. And many of the most suitable test subjects are too ill to be interviewed.

In addition, researchers have attempted to provide an independent source of veridical stimuli. Putting that another way, they have been installing shelves above the beds where the most seriously ill patients are treated. The shelves are well above eye level, and the upper surface contains one of several clear images. The image can be seen only if you were to climb a chair or ladder and peer over the top—or you were floating high above yourself in an out-of-body experience.

The main study to do this recorded more than 2,000 cardiac arrests in which 330 of the patients survived. Only 140 of them were well enough to discuss their experience (and agreed to) soon afterward. Nine of those reported something that ranked as a near-death experience on the NDE scale. Two subjects reported an out-of-body experience. One of those became too ill to continue the interview. The final subject had been in a bed that did not have one of the veridical-stimulus shelves above it.

> "That lucidity might give them control over what they dream about."

So the search for verifiable data continues.

Another avenue for studying NDEs is to look closely at similar phenomena that occur at times other than grave illness. Many of the things involved in NDEs, such as the feeling of floating, meeting other-worldly beings, and being outside the body, are features of various dream states. For example, a lucid dream is one where the dreamer wakes up in the dream. They know they are dreaming but their body is still asleep. That lucidity might give them control over what they dream about. Unshackled from reality, they can do literally whatever they want. That control is not always total, however, and the dream may continue with the dreamer experiencing as a first-person story, guided by the subconscious. Perhaps it is a bit of nightmare, and the dreamer finds they have trouble escaping—they can't wake up.

Dreaming is another sphere of inquiry that is fraught with difficult problems. The level of awareness can vary. In an idle daydream or a light snooze, a person can easily become aware of their mental and physical state, only their attention is elsewhere for a time. In a deep dream, the person is seldom aware of their mental state— they do not know they are dreaming—and if they were to become aware, they still do not have control over their physical state. During REM sleep, the body is paralyzed (almost). The best reason we can think of is so that people do not act out their dreams.

> The level of awareness can vary. In an idle daydream or a light snooze, a person can easily become aware of their mental and physical state, only their attention is elsewhere for a time.

Many people suffer from a condition called sleep paralysis, where they wake from deep sleep but find that the body is still paralyzed (temporarily). Some of them report sensing the presence of another being in the room as they lie there incapable of moving. Again, no one really knows what is happening here, but a good theory is that the voluntary motor controls—the ability to move muscles—have been shut down during a dream and are yet to start up again. However, the waking brain has become aware of its body. This involves collecting a host of sensory inputs and associating them into a mental model of the body's posture. Yet, there is a disconnect between this sensory model and the motor system used to control posture. One of the key inputs on posture comes from the muscles themselves. But this component is missing from the associative model in the brain. As a result, the person's brain has two competing perceptions of where the body is—one from the relaxed muscles, the other from the other sensory information. Consequently, one of those models is perceived to be outside of the body and is felt as another presence nearby.

> " However, the waking brain has become aware of its body. This involves collecting a host of sensory inputs and associating them into a mental model of the body's posture. "

So there are a lot of conflicting theories and information about what the near-death experience can mean. Is it evidence of the soul leaving the body and heading for the next phase of its existence, or is it an artifact of the dying brain? Or could it be both?

THE
BIG ANSWER

When faced with a patient in mortal danger of dying from cardiac arrest, medical staff will not pause the treatment so they can wire up the poor unfortunate to a brain scanner. Understandably, their attentions are elsewhere. However, what they might find would be intriguing.

In lieu of people, NDE researchers have been killing hundreds of lab rats instead. They induce cardiac arrest in the rodents and record the brain activity. While the rest of the body becomes less active, the brain does the opposite. The activity intensifies before reaching a peak, known as the death spike. Then it fades away. The rat has died.

Brain activity increases as death approaches.

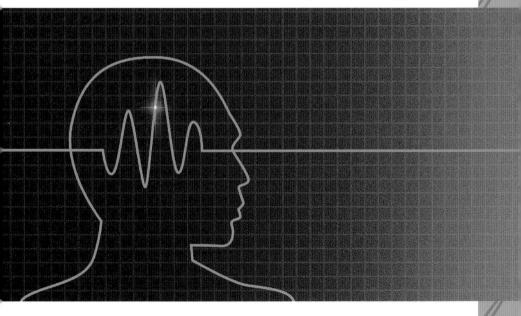

Death spikes have been recorded in humans too, albeit by chance and in a less systematic way. Is this spike the near-death experience taking place? And if so, what is the brain doing?

> 66 This causes an elevation in brain activity in the middle of the brain—a region called the "temporoparietal junction." 99

Brain activities similar to death spikes are linked to a condition called "hypercarbia." This is when the levels of carbon dioxide in the blood get very high. Hypercarbia is the result of not breathing. That also causes hypoxia— not enough oxygen—but it is the presence of the carbon dioxide that seems to be causing the change in brain activity. The brain controls our breathing rate by measuring the amount of carbon dioxide in the blood. If there is a lot, you will breathe more quickly to get rid of it. If the level is low, your breathing is suppressed— and your brain does not get the oxygen it needs. There is a simple way of avoiding this: stick to breathing air and not any other gases that you might have around. However, controlled breathing techniques can be learned that induce hypercarbia and create spiritual experiences. This is the kind of thing the seers, fakirs, and shamans in traditional cultures might do.

So close to death, after breathing has stopped, the level of carbon dioxide in the blood rises. This causes an elevation in brain activity in the middle of the brain—

a region called the "temporoparietal junction."
All regions of the brain are rather mysterious. They
seldom do just one thing, and most appear to have
a hand in a wide range of seemingly unconnected
functions. The temporoparietal junction is linked to
the sense of self as it draws on information from the
senses and emotion centers to create an ever-changing
status report of who you are, how you're feeling, and
what makes you distinct from everything else. The
area also includes a speech center called "Wernicke's
area," which is linked to the associative requirements
of language. The meaning of language is not fixed, but
relates to a wide range of associated factors. Our brain
appears to be figuring out what it all means here.

> " They return but have been
> transformed by the experience. "

So the death spike may indicate a brain that is being
overwhelmed by a dire situation. The body is failing,
and the brain is trying to make sense of what is
happening. All of its data (for want of a better word)
is being passed to the temporoparietal junction as
it searches for an answer. Perceptions of self are
heightened so it feels even more "real" than real
life, important memories are recalled from the past
to see if they hold an answer, the mental map of the
body begins to fragment as different bits of sensory
information stop reaching the brain—and the self
becomes distinct from the body.

The hero story gets real.

As we have seen this kind of experience is not limited to near death. However, something that NDEs do have in common that other experiences do not is the story. A typical NDE involves a feeling of leaving the body—although not necessarily seeing it happen—and entering a strange world. The experiencers are reluctant at first, but after being encouraged to proceed by a mentor figure, they strike out on a journey where they discover new things about themselves and the people in their lives. Finally, they reach a point where they have the choice to proceed or return home to everyday life. They return but have been transformed by the experience.

Reading that back it sounds like the skeleton plot of a movie—anything from *The Karate Kid* to *Superman*—and failing that a Greek hero epic. This kind of story has been described as the monomyth. We've been telling it to each other for millennia. So is an NDE the brain casting its stimuli into the simplest and most powerful story—our own personal action movie? Or is the prevalence of the monomyth in human culture indicative of something deeper? Does it explain some core feature of consciousness?

This is where the materialist view of NDE diverges with the alternative ones. A materialist seeks to understand an NDE in terms of the scientific laws that govern our universe. The body, alive or dead, is made of the same materials. The transit of energy through a living body is just different from its behavior in a dead one. The alternative views promote the idea that at death some mental entity leaves the body. A traditional Western monotheistic view is that this is the soul entering paradise—or perhaps the opposite. Another version—some might say the Eastern concept—has the soul losing its identity as it joins some kind of collective consciousness shared by all things.

> " Representation is what we can perceive outside our body. Our Will thinks about waving a hand, and we see that hand move. "

> " The self perceives both those aspects, but when we see someone else waving back, we can perceive only the Representation of the wave, not the Will that created it. "

The German philosopher Arthur Schopenhauer had something to say about the latter idea in the early nineteenth century. "Every man takes the limits of his own field of vision to be the limits of the world." He is saying that a person's knowledge is limited by the scope of their senses, which we can apply to an NDE. We only understand what is happening in terms of our past life—the content of our brain. Schopenhauer used the content of his brain to reinterpret the two aspects of reality as Will and Representation. Every object has Will, he said. We might also call this consciousness. Will is perceived only from within objects—so only you are conscious of yourself. Representation is what we can perceive outside our body. Our Will thinks about waving a hand, and we see that hand move. The self perceives both those aspects, but when we see someone else waving back, we can perceive only the Representation of the wave, not the Will that created it.

So looking down on our body during a near-death experience is akin to the Will perceiving it as a separate Representation. Schopenhauer explained that space and time are Representations, just like the body or the hospital bed, so in effect, your Will is timeless and everywhere—and that means the same single Will fills the entire universe. Perhaps Schopenhauer would have seen a near-death experience as a unification with the universal Will. That said, he held out no hope of his identity surviving death, but rather it would dissipate into a cold, uncaring universe.

Despite its gloomy end note, Schopenhauer's idea sums up the central mystery about NDEs. Does consciousness persist after the brain has apparently ceased to function—even for a short time? In which case, "where" is it?

Q7

CAN **THE MIND** LIVE WITHOUT A **BODY**?

We a born mindless—at least I was, and it is a safe bet that you were too. It was not until we started to play hide and seek, and crucially, start to be good at it, that we can be sure our minds were in place. An infant knows quite a lot, but a game of hide and seek will expose something that they do not know. In the first few games, a hider might simply cover their eyes. They cannot see and therefore they cannot be seen. This player draws no distinction between the content of his or her thoughts and those of the others in the game. If they cannot see themselves, neither can the seekers. The hiding place is perfect. Of course, they are found quite quickly, and they learn quite quickly that what they may know is not the same as what anyone else knows. They have started to formulate their "theory of mind," the first step in developing full consciousness.

When our body becomes irrevocably unconscious, when the mind has gone and can never return, we are generally considered to be dead.

Understanding the human mind, or at least examining it, is part of life. And our views of it are integral to our considerations of death. When our body becomes irrevocably unconscious, when the mind has gone and can never return, we are generally considered to be dead. There is a grey area concerning the continuous vegetative state, when a person is awake but seemingly not conscious. This shows that the body can live without the mind, but is the mind distinct from the body? Can the two be separated?

We can begin by wondering where consciousness, or the mind, resides and what its link is with the body. It is perhaps hard to take that question seriously—obviously it is in the head. At least that is what you have always been told, but what does you heart say about it?

The ancient Egyptians had a different view. To them the brain was some kind of radiator. All it was for was shedding the heat from the blood. If it became damaged, the animal spirits that controlled the body would build up into a hot feverish frenzy, and we would die. In ancient Egypt, the seat of thought was the heart—and we still use that organ to symbolize our emotional lives.

These kinds of cultural vestiges are what the French philosopher Michel Foucault called the "archaeology of thought." He, like many a post-war French philosopher, was interested in understanding what the essence of humanity was. Foucault began to mistrust the question. Human nature, he reasoned, did not have to be some kind of eternal axiom. There was obviously a time when there was no such thing as a human and no such thing as human nature.

> " These kinds of cultural vestiges are what the French philosopher Michel Foucault called the "archaeology of thought." "

Foucault's proposition is that our current ideas about what it is to be a conscious human have arisen from many developments throughout history. Can we put ourselves in the mind of an ancient Egyptian? Where did they place their inner voice, the one that does the thinking, and their mind's eye? Was it in the chest? Also, did they even consider their thoughts to be entirely their own, or was it the voice of a god or demon (variable according to mood)? Were ancient Egyptians even conscious in the way that we understand it today?

Ancient Egyptians thought the soul traveled to the afterlife on a boat.

131

The ancient Greeks certainly believed their mental lives were at the whim of supernatural forces. A great fear was that the Furies, spirits who lived in the underworld, would emerge to terrorize you,

66 The ancient Greeks certainly believed their mental lives were at the whim of supernatural forces. 99

forcing you to murder and do generally awful things. Were the Furies literally old ladies who live underground? We can safely assume not. Instead, they were the Hellenic way of describing evil thoughts that overwhelmed the vengeful.

Where did these Furies reside in the body? Plato's view was that the human body harbored three souls. The one that governed animal appetites and urges was located in the liver. The emotions and passions were controlled by the heart, while wisdom was at the command of the head. Philosophers like Plato were ruled by the head, courageous warriors were run from the heart, while everyone else (Plato was less than egalitarian) lived at the whim of their livers.

Another Greek, the much jollier Democritus, was another believer in the tripartite soul. Democritus, sometimes remembered as the Laughing Philosopher because he chose to giggle at the universe, which he said was aimless and pointless, is best remembered for developing the first working theory of atoms. We won't go into that now, but according to Democritus, everything was made of atoms, including the soul. He believed that while water atoms were smooth and slippery, and fire atoms were sharp and spiked, the atoms of the soul were diffuse and imperceptible. They permeated the three organs in question and at death simply drifted away. So according to this influential Greek, the soul had physical form but became disordered at death just like the rest of the body.

Plato   *Democritus*

The ancient Greek attitude toward sleep also gives us an idea of how their human nature was different from ours. According to Homer, sleep and death were "two twins of a winged race." Overseen by the two sons of Nyx, the god of night, sleep was a halfway step toward death. It was ruled by Hypnos and was caused by blood, which was cooled by the dark and was draining. If the blood failed to return with the dawn, the sleeper would fall into the hands of Hypnos's brother, Thanatos, the god of death. Even something as straightforward as going to bed was fraught with risk.

> " Most of the nerve tracts leading from the eyes and other senses seemed to join the brain at the front, and so the forward ventricles were deemed to hold the power of perception. "

As the first millennia CE dawned, the first putative steps toward a scientific approach were being made. Galen, a Greco-Roman doctor, who learned a great deal about anatomy while serving as a medic at a gladiatorial arena, was the first to show that the brain was the body's main control center, and the seat of the mind.

That is where it has remained ever since. Early Christian scholars attempted to pinpoint where in the brain the soul

> " Avicenna wanted to know what his mind would be like if the flow of common sense was interrupted. "

was located. Again, the number three was seen as important, this time to represent the Holy Trinity. The problem was that the brain has four fluid-filled spaces, or ventricles, which were deemed to hold the "animal spirits" that controlled the brain and the body. No matter, though, the forward two were paired and so counted as one. Most of the nerve tracts leading from the eyes and other senses seemed to join the brain at the front, and so the forward ventricles were deemed to hold the power of perception. The middle ventricle held memories—later updated to include reason as well. The business end was at the rear (actually the bottom), with that ventricle controlling responses.

By the tenth century, Avicenna, a scholar from Persia, had a good idea. It was basically common sense. Avicenna's version of mind had sensory information arriving at the front of the brain. There it was combined into a single stream of information, which he called the "common sense." The common sense then moved to the middle ventricle where it met with reason—and the appropriate response was commanded. Then it continued to the rear ventricle, where it was laid down as a memory to be used in future to help understand the common sense in the future.

Avicenna wanted to know what his mind would be like if the flow of common sense was interrupted. He used his uncommon good sense to perform what would now be described as a thought experiment. He imagined a man who was blindfolded and his ears plugged so he could not see nor hear a thing. The man was suspended in the air by some effortless method—he was not strung up, but his arms and legs were stretched out so he could not touch any part of his own body. Avicenna called the guy the "Flying Man." Avicenna wondered what was it like to be the Flying Man. Without any input from the outside world, was there anything in his head? Avicenna decided there was. The mind and body were separate entities, with some kind of magical—at least unknown—connection.

This idea is now known as "**dualism**," and it is Rene Descartes who is remembered as its chief proponent. Descartes was a prolific fellow, despite having a shaky start in life—or perhaps thanks to it. The young Rene was a sickly child but bright, and so the Jesuits who ran his boarding school in Paris allowed him to stay in bed for much of the day. As an adult,

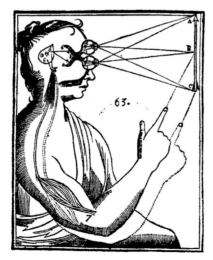

Descartes continued the habit. It is reported that he formulated his ideas of geometric algebra while watching a fly buzz from point to point on his bedroom ceiling. For the uninitiated, geometric algebra is a technique that link equations with lines—most of us would simply call it using graphs.

Descartes's view of the mind and body

As well as being a math whizz, Descartes is also remembered for his immortal phrase, "I think, therefore, I am." And yes, this idea was bed-based as well. Descartes reported that he awoke from a dream and began his day (most likely in bed) only to find that he woke up a second time. The first experience was all a dream. Descartes was left wondering whether he would wake up again. Perhaps his entire life so far was a dream?

It was this doubt that proved his savior. What proof did he have that anything really existed? His body could be in the control of another being or force; he could not disprove it. But the very fact that he was filled with doubt told him that he could be sure of one thing, and one thing only—himself. Only a conscious mind could doubt its own existence.

Descartes saw a clear division between the body and the mind. The body worked largely by reflex, a flesh robot that carried on according to a preset program. The mind could take control when necessary to direct proceedings. Descartes's version of the mind was immaterial—it was not made of anything physical, and it could not be detected. He proposed that it interfaced with the physical world through the pineal body. The pineal body is a gland that hangs out from the bottom of the brain. While the brain (like the rest of the body) is bilateral—it has a mirror image on each side of the body—the pineal gland appeared to be unusually singular. The pineal body is involved in secreting the chemicals that control mood and the day-to-day rhythms of the body. However, Descartes described it as the seat of the soul—a "third eye" that connected to the mystical realm beyond the senses. According to him, the

> " Descartes's version of the mind was immaterial—it was not made of anything physical, and it could not be detected. "

soul communicated with the body via minute twitches and pulsations running through the pineal gland.

Baruch Spinoza, a Dutch philosopher, was one of the first to oppose Descartes's division between the mind and body. To Spinoza, there could be no difference because everything in the universe was part of the same Nature. The mind was as much part of Nature as the body, and while he was at it, Spinoza declared that the whole of history was predetermined. It did not matter what you thought, learned, or reasoned, everything just happened because it was necessary to maintain nature in a state of perfection.

So, by seventeenth century, those who had time to think about it—most had a lot more pressing needs, like simply warding off starvation—were presented with two options concerning the mind: it was a supernatural soul that existed outside of physical reality (and could persist after death), or it was an extension of the body, as much a functional unit as an arm or eyeball. Has much changed since?

Descartes *Spinoza*

THE
BIG ANSWER

Hot on the heels of Descartes and Spinoza came John Locke. His famous contribution was the idea that at birth, the human mind was a tabula rasa, or a clean slate. According the Locke, the entire content of a person's mind—their memories, knowledge, and ability to reason—is the product of experience and education.

There were disagreements, of course. Some people suggested that certain elements of knowledge were innate, but the idea was the body was ruled by internal mental processes, which were perceptible only to an individual.

However, in the 1950s, a zoologist called B. F. Skinner threw even this into doubt. His field became known as radical behaviorism, and it was radical because it put an end to all the high-minded philosophical conjecture that came before it.

66 Skinner invented an experimental apparatus, now known as a Skinner box … The box was fitted with actuators that gave rewards and punishments to the occupant. 99

Skinner invented an experimental apparatus, now known as a Skinner box. An animal was placed inside— Skinner used pigeons, but the point was a box could be made to suit any animal if needed. The box was fitted with actuators that gave rewards and punishments to the occupant. Skinner used his boxes to show that animals as "dumb" as a pigeon could learn complex tasks, equally complex as had been taught to "intelligent" species such as chimps.

Skinner chose not to interpret these results as proof that pigeons were as clever as apes. Instead, he did something much more radical. He said his work showed that mental processes, intelligent or otherwise, were irrelevant to learning. The only evidence that was required to explain the learning process were the observable behaviors.

Pigeons, clever or dumb?

Every action was simply the consequence of a stimulus. Whether, animals, including humans, had mental processes or not, they were not involved in learning.

Help! What's going on now? Is the mind an illusion?

For the next fifteen years or so, no one could say it was not—although the massed legion of neuroscientists seldom agreed with that radical behaviorist notion. What was needed was a physical trace of a mental process.

That was achieved in the late 1960s by Eric Kandel, who won the Nobel Prize for the discovery in 2000. Kandel revealed the chemical changes that occur in brain cells as they form memories. Memories are stored (somehow) as "memory networks" of brain cells. This idea was summed up as "Cells that fire together, wire together." The search is still on to pinpoint an actual memory in the brain. This is partly because brain scanners cannot look closely enough at living cells in the brain, and partly because a single memory is not stored in one place but is built from several fragments. These in turn are associated with other memories, and so on. The chemistry of the brain reflects a physical link to a mental process, but the code contained in all those chemical shifts and electrical pulses that are used to create a conscious thought is still beyond our understanding.

> " Kandel revealed the chemical changes that occur in brain cells as they form memories. "

66 David Chalmers, an
Australian philosopher,
chose to look at the
problems of consciousness
from another direction.
He imagined philosophical
zombies. 99

David Chalmers, an Australian philosopher, chose to
look at the problems of consciousness from another
direction. He imagined philosophical zombies. These
are not the mutilated undead corpses of the popular
imagination. From outside they look completely normal.
They behave completely appropriately, but they have
no consciousness. Their actions occur without a
mental component. If Chalmers had not told us they
were zombies, we could never tell. Even cutting them
in half—don't worry they have no awareness, and are
therefore incapable of suffering—reveals that the brain
is completely intact and apparently normal in every way.

Chalmers's thought experiment is meant to highlight
how hard, perhaps impossible, it is to compare two
people's consciousness. If we were to climb into
someone else's consciousness, would we see the world
differently? Although the sky is blue, would your host
consciousness represent that as a different color to the
one that you see it as? It is all blue, as we've said, but
what evidence is there that blue is always the same
from one mind to the next?

What color do you see?

Chalmers extends this idea. The mind is produced by the physical brain, but its consciousness produces qualia—subjective qualities, feelings, and sensations— that have no physical basis. He proposes that a brain of a certain size and form will always be conscious. Therefore, his zombies can't exist. These beings have a perfectly good human brain inside, and thus they must have consciousness. However, that consciousness does not belong to the brain as such but is an awareness of a wider universal phenomenon. We are back to Spinoza.

To balance the books, kind of, we will end by looking more at how our brains produce consciousness. There is no consciousness center at the front of the brain. As with most higher functions, the brain works through association, drawing together inputs from all over the place. Researchers are building complex multidimensional models that are attempts at understanding the links between the different brain activities and how these may influence one another.

However, the sensory and motor cortices are perhaps easier to understand—and that is why they were some of the first regions to be identified on the brain's functional map. The sensory cortex collects inputs from touch sensors all over the body.

> "The result appeared to show that the motor cortex was already preparing to send the signal to the muscles before the subject decided to make the movement."

Alongside it is the motor cortex. This will send commands to the muscles in response to what the body is touching. For our purposes, the bit in the middle is "consciousness." The brain is sending signals as electric pulses, and just before the motor cortex sends out a signal to the body, its electric field elevates slightly. This is called the "readiness potential." In the 1980s, researchers wanted to know more about how long it took for the brain to think about voluntary movements. Their results were somewhat unexpected. Not everyone agrees with the methodology used, but test subjects were asked to note the exact time they decided to move a finger, and this was compared with the activity of the brain. The result appeared to show that the motor cortex was already preparing to send the signal to the muscles before the subject decided to make the movement. At the very least, this indicated that our awareness lags behind our decision making by a fraction of a second. At most, it indicated that all of our actions are controlled subconsciously, and our consciousness merely gives the illusion that we are in command of our bodies. We do not exercise free will.

There is a third possibility. The body is running on automatic most of the time, and the mind only steps in to veto certain actions. Some have called this state of affairs "free won't." All in all, it is something Rene Descartes may have recognized.

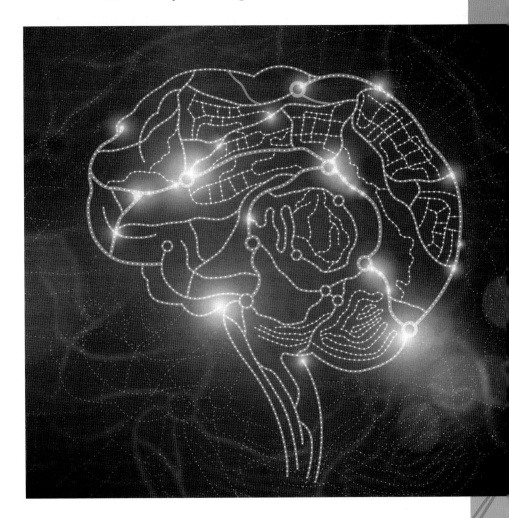

Q8

IS **IMMORTALITY** A **GOOD THING?**

> Who wants to live forever? I'm not talking just a few centuries; I mean forever. The heat death of the universe is scheduled for 22 billion years from now—I know not long is it?—and you immortals will still be there. The universe will be cold and diffuse. All matter will be spread so thin that there will be no interactions. Nothing will happen, ever again. And you will be there to see it.

Of course the sun will have blown up long before then, turning Earth into a seared lump of rock. We should perhaps assume that you were killed in that event. For the purposes of this chapter, let's assume that an immortal person never dies of natural causes but could be killed by accident. Perhaps it was a car accident, a parachuting accident, or being obliterated by quark torpedoes during the attack of the Vorgons in the seventy-ninth century.

> " If that is the immortality being offered, would you take it? "

If that is the immortality being offered, would you take it? Perhaps first you should take a lesson from Greek mythology: the goddess of the dawn, Eos, captured Tithonus, a handsome Trojan, as her lover. She then appealed to Zeus, the king of the gods, to make Tithonus immortal so the couple could enjoy an eternal love affair. Zeus agreed but in so doing taught Eos a lesson. Tithonus became immortal but kept on aging. He gradually lost the ability to move and eventually turned into a cicada, forever burbling but never, ever dying.

So let's add another condition to our immortality: we never get any older physically—or perhaps we settle at some vigorous stage of development and stay there for eternity. That sounds a lot better, doesn't it?

Alchemists certainly thought so, and along with the philosopher's stone—needed to ensure a healthy income of gold for the eternity to come—they searched nature for the elixir. The term "elixir" is derived from the Arabic word for "stuff of miracles," but it is generally regarded as a drinkable substance. So here we are, would you have a drop of the elixir?

Searching for wealth and immortality

Before you answer, there are many ways of thinking about immortality, be it through identity, ethics and values, biology, or even probability. Let's see if any of them sway your answer from a yes to a no.

> " If identity is the sum total of your thoughts and memories over time, then your identity is always changing. "

Some philosophy first. While the immortal body does not age, the mind surely does. Philosophers continue to wrestle with the concept of identity. John Locke, for example, pondered what happens when the minds of a prince and pauper swap places. Does the identity travel with the minds or stay with the bodies? Castle courtiers would attend to the prince's body, obviously, but the transmitted prince now living in squalor would certainly hope that he was still a royal.

In the 1980s, the British philosopher Derek Parfit updated the thought experiment. Captain Kirk is being beamed down to a planet, but something goes wrong with the transporter. Despite Scotty's best efforts, two Captain Kirks arrive on the surface at precisely the same time. (I think this actually happened in one way or another in an episode of *Star Trek*—Kirk had to fight Kirk, and Kirk won, like he always does.) Anyway, Parfit wanted to understand which one is the original Kirk and which one is the copy. Perhaps it is neither.

Put your back into it!

If identity is the sum total of your thoughts and memories over time, then your identity is always changing. You are already a different person after starting to read this chapter. So both the Kirks are different from the one that left the *Enterprise*, and now that both have separate experiences, they are developing separate identities.

So as you live forever, who you are is changing. In a million years, your identity will be remarkably changed. Is it you who is living forever or a succession of different beings?

> " All of your identities are connected along a timeline, and they all share a common goal—your survival. "

All of your identities are connected along a timeline, and they all share a common goal—your survival. But if that is assured by your immortality, what is it that you are living for? The German philosopher Martin Heidegger said that the prospect of eventual death was the driving force behind the project that was a human life. To live authentically, you had to understand that the many goals you set for yourself throughout your life would not ward off death forever. That might alter what you choose to do but you should do it anyway.

In the *Myth of Sisyphus*, the absurdist philosopher Albert Camus put it all another way. His book described the "paradox of the absurd," which stemmed from the observation that even if a person reasons that their life—ending in inescapable death—is futile, they still maintain that it has some value. Sisyphus was condemned by the gods to push a rock up a hill every day, only to see it roll back down to the bottom, and so he started again. In Camus's version, the hero finds happiness in this thankless act. Camus is urging us to embrace the meaninglessness of our own lives (hopefully more varied than that of Sisyphus). We should not, says Camus, evade the absurdity with clever, logic-based systems to create a meaning.

What would immortals do? They are not going to die. Are their lives any less futile? They can set goals—for pleasure or for virtue—and be certain of achieving them, eventually. So why bother starting now? They have eternity.

Also, what project is worth doing? Curing illness is no longer a noble career—nobody gets ill. Nurturing children is not required, immortals do not need to breed. Even physical pleasures like food would begin to wane after the first few centuries. This immortality is beginning to sound like a waste of time.

THE
BIG ANSWER

First off, is it actually possible to life forever? Theoretically, there are life forms that are immortal—at least they have not died yet. The organisms in question are those that reproduce by simply breaking in half, or casting off a part of their bodies to start a new individual. Life forms on this list include bacteria and yeasts, strawberries, and certain kinds of jellyfish-like things called "hydroids."

These organisms are a bit like the Captain Kirks from our thought experiment. They break in two—often in unequal parts—and one can be seen as the original parents and the other as a daughter. Barring predation and accidental death, it is possible for the parents to keep on living forever—unlikely but possible.

> 66 All identical twins are clones in that they share the same genome, but not all clones are twins. 99

Humans do not reproduce in this way. The very thought is rather off putting. However, would cloning ourselves result in immortality? All identical twins are clones in that they share the same genome, but not all clones are twins. A clone of you would always be younger and therefore have a different identity. Just because they share all your genes, they do not know what you know. Also their physical appearance, although similar to yours, would be different due to variance in diet and stress as they developed. There are plenty of other ways a clone is significantly different from its parent, but suffice it to say cloning is not the answer to the quest for immortality.

Preparing for a long life

For those seeking immortality there is a registered charity that can help, the Immortalist Society. This was set up in the 1960s to support those who wished to be **cryogenically** frozen on death—and then resurrected when medical science could manage it. The techniques used to preserve the body are complex to say the least, and there is no evidence that they work. Medical technology cannot raise the dead yet. Assuming the preservation works as intended, the corpse (sometimes just the head) is kept below -94° Fahrenheit (-70°C) in liquid nitrogen. "Patients" are no doubt aware of the low probability that they will be given a second life, but they have time on their side.

> They take many hours to physically break down. However, after a few minutes—depending on first aid and other conditions, this can be hours, but time is against us—the deoxygenated cells have passed a point of no return.

It is a misconception that body cells—especially those in the brain—die within minutes once the supply of blood ends. They take many hours to physically break down. However, after a few minutes—depending on first aid and other conditions, this can be hours, but time is against us—the deoxygenated cells have passed a point of no return. If blood rich in oxygen was pumped back into the cells, they would be destroyed by what is called "reperfusion injuries." It is the attempt to save life that kills it, but there is nothing else that can be done. Yet, that is. Those frozen patients are ready for when there is a fix.

There is danger everywhere, all the time.

Let's say all the obstacles have been overcome and you are immortal and happy to be so. Your life would be without limits. Or perhaps the opposite. What are the chances of being run over the next time you cross the road? Quite low, negligible, one hopes. However, in a world of immortals the likelihood of dying in a car accident is something close to certainty. Perhaps cars and roads are no longer a feature of the future world in which you are living. Perhaps you have also escaped from the dying Earth and have plenty of time to spare until the end of the universe. Even so activities that carry tiny but measurable risks could become paralyzing for an immortal. There are so many dangers that eventually you will be killed by one. The only solution would be to live one moment at a time, in the full knowledge that a personal catastrophe could happen any time. That seems quite a nice way to live, and you would have plenty of time to get used to it. However, something has happened to your immortal self— you no longer want to live forever.

66 Perhaps cars and roads are no longer a feature of the future world in which you are living. 99

There is another, safer way to live forever. A mind upload. Read on to find out if that has already happened to you.

Q9

IS **LIFE REAL** OR A **SIMULATION**?

THE
BIG ANSWER

Obviously nobody knows—they would have told us by now if they did. However, astronomers have had a good look. A simulation will have limits, and in terms of a universe, that would be limits on matter and energy. The place to look for an upper limit of energy is in the ultra-powerful cosmic rays that permeate the universe. If they all cut off at the same level, that might indicate our universe is preprogrammed. What will we do if it turns out we are all computer characters?

Q10

WHY DO WE HAVE TO DIE?

> 66 Eventually the body will fail, its life will end, and death takes over. 99

Life is able to work against the inexorable flow of time. It can build brand new bodies, unblemished by accidents or disease. Why is it incapable of making a body stay forever young?

The body picks up bruises and scratches all the time, and when young it is able to fix them, for the most part. All but the most severe injuries and damage will fade with time, becoming, by themselves, negligible. However, accumulated over a lifetime, these acquired injuries will begin to have a nonnegligible effect on the body as a whole, causing chronic problems and lowering the body's defenses against the constant onslaught of life. Gradually the body begins to weaken, ceases to work as well as it once did, and the cumulative "dis-eases" continue to mount. There is no way to reverse them all. Eventually the body will fail, its life will end, and death takes over.

Most of us would accept this rather lyrical description of aging as fact. However, what drives aging is not wear and tear by itself. Living things appear to actively age, and they all do it at different speeds.

Q11

IS THERE AN
AFTERLIFE?

A mayfly close to death

Why is it that an adult mayfly lives only for a week or two? (The idea that it lives for a day is a myth, but its days can be numbered on two hands, and perhaps a foot, too.) Is it because its fragile fluttering form is prone to injury as it blunders through the pond-side undergrowth? Is it because it does not eat—the digestive tract is pumped full of air to aid buoyancy—and so lacks the energy to restore its battered body? Yes and no. It just does not need to live any longer.

What about the quahog? Forget what you've heard about the longest living animals—it is not the giant tortoise or blue whale or donkey. The oldest animal with a confirmed age was a hard clam, or quahog, called Ming. He/she (clams are hermaphrodites) was dredged up from the seabed near to Iceland in 2006. Researchers were able to calculate the mollusc's age by counting the growth rings in its shell. Ming was 507 years old. He/she had hatched from an egg in 1499, just a couple of years after John Cabot had

> " Researchers were able to calculate the mollusc's age by counting the growth rings in its shell. Ming was 507 years old. "

sailed past (not too far away) en route to "discovering" North America. However, poor old Ming became a martyr to science and was killed by the examination. Undoubtedly Ming had the benefit of a double-shelled suit of armor to protect him/her from the injuries that befall all bodies. However, is that enough to ensure a life of five centuries? Or was Ming just very lucky, having found a safe spot on the seabed?

Related quahogs have been found that are approaching their 300th birthdays, so Ming may have been exceptional, but luck was not the overriding factor.

Some animals live in very harsh environments that would kill the quahog, the mayfly, and humans in short order. The cute-sounding water bears (they are also known as moss piglets) are actually microscopic arthropods that were discovered only when biologists started to look in rain puddles and other temporary pools of water. The critters also live in icy oceans, on top of mountains, and in hot springs. Basically, water bears can survive wherever there is a scrap of moisture. Inevitably, however, these ephemeral habitats will disappear as the water dries up. The water bears, or tardigrades (meaning "slow walker"), will lose their homes. However, they are ready for it. The animal draws its eight legs into its body and forms a tough encysted form. There is no sign of life, there is precious little water or oxygen left in the body, and metabolism has ceased. Biologists call this kind of activity "**cryptobiosis**."

A water bear does not need to die.

For all intents and purposes the animal acts as if it were dead.

And it can continue to be dead for decades, presumably forever. The cyst can withstand extremes of temperature, well beyond the conditions found on Earth. When going about its day-to-day business, the water bear is 85 percent water. The cyst is just 3 percent water. It can be squashed by pressures that exceed those of the deepest ocean trenches, and it can even cope with radiation doses thousands of times higher than what would be fatal to a human. To illustrate the water bears' toughness, in 2007, a crew of encysted water bears were flown into space and left outside in the vacuum for ten days. On return, the invertebrate explorers were revived. Two-thirds of them had survived their journey.

> " There is no sign of life, there is precious little water or oxygen left in the body, and metabolism has ceased. "

If aging is simply the result of the body getting old, water bears appear to be able to stop that process whenever they need to.

If aging is not a universal feature of life, then what differentiates it from any other life-threatening condition? In a medical context, aging is just another terminal disease.

Name a disease. Off the top of our heads, many of us would perhaps opt for something contagious, such as chicken pox, Ebola, or malaria. There are other diseases, of course— cancer, mental illness, dementia.

Infectious diseases are caused by pathogens. We might call them germs or bugs, and they include things like viruses, bacteria, fungi, amoebas, and even microscopic worms. Not all of these things are pathogens. Far from it; most are harmless to us and indeed perform a useful role in the body. Take bacteria, for example. The idea of a bacterial infection fills people with dread. However, for every cell in your body—there are about a trillion—there are ten bacterial cells in there as well. Most of them are in the gut or on the skin. They are minute in volume compared to body cells so

A pathogen

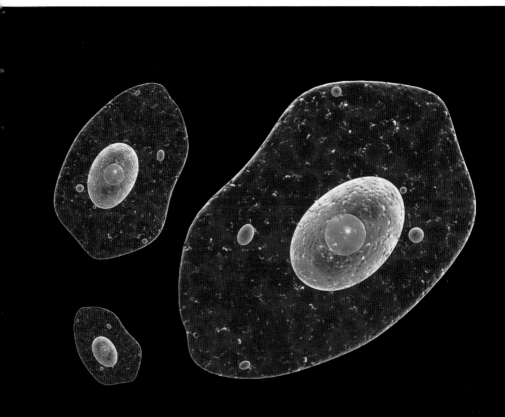

they do not come close to matching your mass, but you are definitely "infected." These bacteria are helpful in that they aid with digestion processes that we find tricky by ourselves, but perhaps most importantly, the "good" bacteria take up all the room, so "bad" bacteria can't find a foothold to launch a disease-causing attack.

Many of the things we associate with illness—aches and pains, high temperature, runny nose, etc.—are in fact the immune response to the pathogen. Blood is filtered through lymph nodes around the body to clear out the invaders. The nodes become tender and swollen in the process. A high temperature is the body increasing its work rate as it declares total war on the invaders.

> 66 Pathogens and parasites are constantly evolving to attack their hosts, who evolve in response to fight them off. 99

The battles are usually won, but at the expense of opportunity. In the natural world, predators will pick off the sick, and strong healthy rivals will outcompete their ailing neighbors.

Many large animals, mostly the ones with K-selective reproductive strategies (think back to chapter 1) have evolved a way of signaling health and vitality. The tail of a peacock, antlers of a stag, or motorbike of a leather-clad rebel are all signals that despite everything the world can throw at them, these individuals have what it takes to win in the battle for survival. They have the energy left over to develop features that not only look good but are also something of a hindrance to survival.

Signaling youth

Biologists call the process by which animals develop these kinds of features the "Red Queen Effect." The red queen in question is the Queen of Hearts from *Through the Looking Glass*, one of Alice's Wonderland adventures. The queen runs hard but stays in the same place, and evolution is also doing the same thing. Pathogens and parasites are constantly evolving to attack their hosts, who evolve in response to fight them off. All this is largely hidden, and so ornamentation has evolved to signal which individuals are winning the unseen battle.

What we regard as a youthful appearance is actually one that is a signal that the body is able to withstand the trials of life. In these terms, an old body can still be "young." Why does the body's ability to renew need to end? For it surely will.

66 In the natural world, predators will pick off the sick, and strong healthy rivals will outcompete their ailing neighbors. 99

THE
BIG ANSWER

The process of aging is not just about getting old. Biology gives it a more precise name: **senescence**. Senescence hits the human body around the age of thirty. After that, the form and function that worked so well until that point begins to gradually deteriorate. It is not the same for everyone. Some people will stay young for a lot longer; others will grow old faster than their age group. This all points to senescence being almost an active process, with the body self destructing, or at least no longer able to reconstruct. There are external factors that also play a part—strong sunlight and cigarette smoke will age the skin, for example—but somehow a point is reached where the body simply stops mending itself. Why is this?

> " The mayfly's senescence starts when it simply runs out of energy supplies, and the body stops working. "

The mayfly's senescence starts when it simply runs out of energy supplies, and the body stops working. A quahog seems to not senesce at all, as also seen in the oldest single living organisms of all—the bristlecone pine. This slow-growing, wizened-looking tree can live for four thousand years or more. It grows very slowly but none of its cells are more than thirty years old!

Cellular senescence is a process that is at work from the very first days of life. It seems that cells have a genetic clock that counts how many times they divide. The clock mechanisms are thought to be structures called "telomeres" on the end of each chromosome. Like a token at a funfair, every time the chromosome is copied (as happens in cell division), one of the telomeres is lost. When there are none left, the cell can no longer divide to renew itself, and it dies.

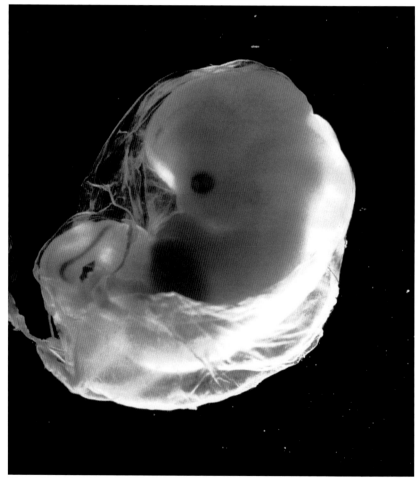

Even in the early days, cells need to die so the fetus can grow.

This process of controlled die-off of certain cells is integral to the development of an embryo. It has been suggested that a similar process limits the ability of the body to renew itself over much longer spans of time, and this is what causes senescence in the organism as a whole.

> The chances of dying before exceeding reproductive age are relatively low, and once you pass the peak of your fertility, your body begins to deteriorate.

Similar theories of aging point to genetic material accruing damage or simply being lost from cells as the organism gets older. It appears that humans lose about half a percent of their DNA from cardiac muscle cells every year. This is a low rate of loss compared to smaller animals, who live shorter lives. Dogs, for example, lose DNA five times faster and live approximately five times less.

This correlation between DNA loss and lifespan points to natural selection being involved somewhere along the line. The chances of dying before exceeding reproductive age are relatively low, and once you pass the peak of your fertility, your body begins to deteriorate. This may be due to the reproductive hormones taking their toll on the body, or it may be an evolved trait. We are just scheduled to die after reproducing. Octopods do it straight away, for example. Once the eggs are hatched and the young are on their way, the mother simply dies, exhausted. Mammals might survive a few years, so they can care for the young, but then they die, too. Humans are unusual in that they live far beyond their reproductive peak. Women experience menopause, and men experience a less well understood andropause, but they do not keel over and die there and then.

In prehistoric times, it would have been relatively rare for individuals to live this long, but those who did would come equipped with a great deal of knowledge accrued over their lifetime. It is thought that the extended lifespan of humans evolved to aid with the survival of grandchildren. The group elders were the only ones old enough to remember the last drought, flood, war, or other rare catastrophe. And they passed on the knowledge of how to get by.

> 66 In prehistoric times, it would have been relatively rare for individuals to live this long, but those who did would come equipped with a great deal of knowledge accrued over their lifetime. 99

Men die younger than women, partly because they are more likely to do dangerous things when young and also because they have slightly less DNA. Their Y chromosome is a toddler compared to the X of a female human cell. A female cell has two Xs while the male cell contains an X and a Y. If a faulty gene is on one X, a female has a spare to supersede it. Males don't have this luxury, and as a result, are at a small but significantly elevated risk of owning a problem gene.

> Men die younger than women, partly because they are more likely to do dangerous things when young and also because they have slightly less DNA.

In the end, the need to survive is trumped by the need to reproduce—at least in biological terms. An immature body devotes all of its resources to growth and repair. Once mature, some of those resources are diverted to secure a mate, produce young, and support it as it grows. No matter how good you are at it—or whether you actually have children or not—that diversion of energy is enough to tip the balance and begin the slow descent into malfunction.

Q11

IS THERE AN
AFTERLIFE?

What happens when we die? Does everything fade to white and then nothing? Most (but not all) religious faiths involve an afterlife, where the mental entity of the believer—from here on out, we'll just stick with "soul"—passes on to another phase of existence.

> Eternal life in a paradise, reincarnation into another body, or a liberation from identity of any kind.

Here are the options: eternal life in a paradise, reincarnation into another body, or a liberation from identity of any kind. Perhaps the most familiar form of afterlife is heaven and hell. The soul leaves the body and enters a nonphysical world—at least one that is not accessible bodily—where it is judged by its deeds. If all is in order, the departed soul goes to heaven, where it enjoys eternal comfort. The rest go to hell and suffer eternal discomfort.

Heaven looks nice. *Hell looks less appealing.*

There are variations on this theme. In Islam, the most faithful are received in a higher level of paradise than those who have adhered to Allah's teachings less in life. There are seven levels of heaven and seven of hell. This idea is also seen in some tellings of Christian dogma, and Catholic teachings talk of a middle zone, or purgatory. Here the righteous souls who have not been properly baptized according the the rules of the Church are cleansed (some say by fire) before ascending to heaven. Although it was never an official part of the Christian faith, those souls that never knew God but committed no earthly sins would be sent to limbo—a nothingness on the edge of hell.

Reincarnation is the afterlife of Hindus, Sikhs, Jains, Buddhists, and several modern religions founded in the West in the last few centuries that were inspired by Eastern tradition. On death, the soul finds its way to another life form just being born. Buddhism does not require an actual transfer of a soul entity for this to happen, but in Hinduism the skull needs to crack in the funeral pyre for the soul to get out.

Souls may take many forms.

The interesting thing about reincarnation is that it means that every life is an afterlife, but it is also a "before life." Where the soul moves to is based on the accumulation of deeds in life. Those who lead the best life can hope to be elevated to an exalted position as a human or other sacred animal. People who have behaved badly will be lowered to the state of vermin or demons.

Reincarnation is not the only option, and is not the goal set of the religious teachings that include the concept. The most faithful and righteous souls are released from the eternal cycle of rebirth, and their identity fades into the egoless contentment that is nirvana.

All these concepts of afterlife require that people do good deeds in life. Without the reward of eternal life of some kind, would the living, bodily world descend further into chaos and selfishness?

> 66 All these concepts of afterlife require that people do good deeds in life. Without the reward of eternal life of some kind, would the living, bodily world descend further into chaos and selfishness? 99

THE
BIG ANSWER

The American philosopher Samuel Scheffler proposes that there is another afterlife. This is the knowledge that your children, friends, and society in general will survive your death. To believe this does not require the convolutions of faith and legend. When loved ones die, you and the rest of humanity continue as normal, so why would it be any different after your own death? There are schools of thought, such as solipsism, which propose that the entire universe exists only inside your consciousness, but there are many arguments against that, and few people would think that when they become unconscious (or even asleep) the universe disappears from existence until they wake up again.

> " When loved ones die, you and the rest of humanity continue as normal, so why would it be any different after your own death? "

Scheffler contends that this form of afterlife is all that is required for the living to adopt moral lives and strive to better themselves and the lot of the human species. He tests this idea by giving you, and you alone, a piece of special knowledge. You will live a normal life and die a natural death, and thirty days after your death the world will suffer a cataclysm (let's say an asteroid strike) that will make the human race become extinct. Remember, you will not suffer from this event, it will not alter the course of your own life in any way, and only you know what lies in store for the rest of the human race once you have died.

In Scheffler's scenario, everybody is gone.

So the question is, what do you do next? Most people find that they would lose the will to continue with the projects of their lives. A medical researcher would stop looking for cures, a politician would stop building a better tomorrow, and in general the reasons to carry on fade away. You personally are not going to be impacted (pun intended) by the extinction, but you do lose out on the certainty of an afterlife. While the questions of soul, heaven and hell, and reincarnation are beyond inquiry, perhaps we can all agree that this kind of afterlife is the one with the most meaning. With it, we are driven to live fair, creative, and constructive lives. Without it, we become lost.

FURTHER INFORMATION

Books

Blackmore, Susan. *Consciousness: A Very Short Introduction.* Oxford, UK: Oxford University Press, 2005.

Lehmann, Devra. *Spinoza: The Outcast Thinker.* South Hampton, NH: Namelos, 2014.

Nagel, Thomas. *What Does It All Mean?: A Very Short Introduction to Philosophy.* Oxford, UK: Oxford University Press, 1987.

Websites

Khan Academy: Biology

https://www.khanacademy.org/science/biology

Watch videos about a wealth of topics in the field of biology. The Khan Academy also gives you the opportunity to take practice quizzes on what you've learned.

The Secret of How Life on Earth Began

http://www.bbc.com/earth/story/20161026-the-secret-of-how-life-on-earth-began

Explore diagrams, photographs, and comprehensive timeline of events on this site from the BBC.

GLOSSARY

biogenesis The idea that life can only come from other life; this understanding of biology stands in contrast to abiogenesis, which says life can arise spontaneously.

cryogenics A descriptive term for using extremely low temperatures to achieve the preservation of life.

cryptobiosis When metabolic processes stop in a plant or animal without causing death.

dualism Rene Descartes's idea that the body and mind are separate.

exobiology A field of science dedicated to the study of life on other planets.

merring An acronym for the conditions of life: movement, excretion, respiration, reproduction, irritability, nutrition, and growth.

Moore's Law Gordon Moore's 1965 idea that computing power would continue to double every year and a half.

senescence In biology, the name for the way that aging causes deterioration of the body and cells.

trophic pyramid Another name for the ecological pyramid, which shows how plants and animals get their energy.

veridical When describing near-death experiences, researchers apply the term "veridical" to any aspect of the experience that can be verified as fact.

INDEX

Entries in boldface are glossary terms.